BITE-SIZE
BIBLE™
ANSWERS

RON RHODES

HARVEST HOUSE PUBLISHERS

EUGENE, OREGON

BITE-SIZE BIBLE™ ANSWERS
Copyright © 2011 by Ron Rhodes
Published by Harvest House Publishers
Eugene, Oregon 97402
www.harvesthousepublishers.com

ISBN 978-0-7369-3730-6 (Trade)
ISBN 978-0-7369-4117-4 (eBook)

To all who seek to be doers of the Word
and not just hearers of the Word

Acknowledgments

I want to give a heartfelt thanks to the team at Harvest House Publishers for their continued commitment to excellence in Christian publishing. I also want to thank my wife, Kerri, and my children, David and Kylie, for their continual support and encouragement while I wrote this book. Without them my work of ministry would truly be an impossible task. They are treasured gifts from the Lord.

Contents

Bite-Size Bible Answers

Good things come in small packages.

I'm not sure who first coined this phrase, but I think there is some truth to it. This book is a small book, a bite-size book. But it is brimming with helpful Bible answers. My goal has been to produce a book that is convenient (small enough to put in a briefcase or a purse) and low-cost, yet loaded with helpful information you can really use. The book provides concise, reliable answers to common questions about the Bible, God, Jesus Christ, the Holy Spirit, humankind, sin, salvation, angels, demons, the prophetic future, the afterlife, and more. I pray that you find this book to be more than a bite-size blessing!

As you read the book, be sure to look up some of the Scripture references I cite. You will increasingly discover, as I have through the years, that the Word of God is a light that guides us (Psalm 119:105), an encourager of our souls (verses 25,37,40,50), and an anchor that keeps us steady (see Hebrews 6:19).

Ron Rhodes
Frisco, Texas, 2010

Part I

The Bible as the Word of God

I

The Inspiration of Scripture

What do we mean when we say the Bible is inspired?

The New Testament Greek word for the process of inspiration literally means "God-breathed" (see 2 Timothy 3:16). Scripture is breathed out by God—it originates from Him—so it is true and inerrant.

When we say the Bible is inspired, we mean that God superintended the human authors so that they composed and recorded His revelation without error, but they used their own individual personalities and even their own unique writing styles. In other words, the Holy Spirit permitted the authors to exercise their own personalities and literary talents even though they wrote under His control and guidance. The result is a perfect and errorless recording of the exact message God desired to give to humankind. This definition of inspiration applies only to the original documents or *autographs*. (An autograph is a manuscript in the author's handwriting.)

**To what extent were the biblical writers
controlled by the Holy Spirit as they wrote?**

In Peter's second letter, he provides a key insight
regarding the human–divine interchange in the process
of inspiration. He writes, "Prophecy [or Scripture] never
had its origin in the will of man, but men spoke from God
as they were carried along by the Holy Spirit" (2 Peter
1:21).

The phrase *carried along* in this verse literally means
"forcefully borne along," like a strong wind carries a ship at
sea (Acts 27:17). Even though human beings were used in
the process of writing down God's Word, they were all literally borne along by the Holy Spirit. God's message did
not originate with the wills of the human authors. He did
not permit the will of sinful human beings to misdirect or
erroneously record His message. Rather, God revealed His
word, and His spokesmen recorded it.

**Were the New Testament writers aware
that their writings were inspired by
God and therefore authoritative?**

Yes. In 1 Corinthians 2:13 the apostle Paul (who wrote
about half of the books in the New Testament) said he
spoke "not in words taught us by human wisdom but in
words taught by the Spirit." Later, Paul affirmed, "What
I am writing to you is the Lord's command" (14:37). He
also referred to his message "not as the word of men, but
as it actually is, the word of God" (1 Thessalonians 2:13).

Doesn't each Bible writer's own bias make the Bible less reliable?

Passionately believing in something does not necessarily force someone to distort history when giving an account of it. In modern times, some of the most reliable reports of the Holocaust were written by Jews who were passionately committed to making sure such genocide never happened again.

The New Testament is not made up of fairy tales. It is based on eyewitness testimony (2 Peter 1:16).

Why does the Bible include four Gospels that have apparent contradictions?

The Gospels may appear to have contradictions, but the apparent contradictions are not genuine. The Gospel accounts do have differences because they are written from different points of view, but they have no actual contradictions.

As we saw earlier, only the original autographs of Scripture are inspired and inerrant. Certainly the copies we have of the original autographs are extremely accurate. But conservative theologians have been very careful to say that the Scriptures, in their original autographs and properly interpreted, are wholly true in everything they teach.

Let's also note that if all four Gospels were exactly the same, critics would accuse the writers of collusion. The fact that the Gospels have differences shows there was no collusion. Rather, we have four different but equally inspired accounts of the same events.

Here's some practical advice: Don't assume that a partial Gospel account is a faulty account. In Matthew 27:5, for example, we are told that Judas hanged himself. In Acts 1:18, we are told that Judas burst open and all his intestines gushed out. These are both partial accounts. Taken together, we get the full picture. Judas hanged himself, and sometime later the rope loosened (or broke) and he fell to the rocks below.

Does science disprove the miracles of the Bible?

Science depends upon observation and replication. Miracles, such as the Incarnation and the resurrection, are unprecedented events. No one can replicate these events in a laboratory. Therefore, science simply cannot be the judge and jury as to whether these events occurred.

The scientific method is useful for studying natural events but not supernatural ones. Just as football stars are speaking outside their field of expertise when they appear on television to tell you what razor you should buy, so scientists are speaking outside their field when they address theological issues like miracles or the resurrection.

We have many good reasons to believe the biblical miracles actually happened. For example, very little time elapsed between Jesus' miraculous public ministry and the publication of the Gospels. Miracle legends could never develop that fast. Also, when the Gospels were written, many eyewitnesses to Jesus' miracles were still alive and would have refuted any untrue miracle accounts (see 1 Corinthians 15:6).

Also, consider the noble character of the men who witnessed these miracles (Peter, James, and John, for example). Such men were not prone to misrepresentation, and they were willing to give up their lives rather than deny their beliefs.

Finally, some of the witnesses of Jesus' miracles were hostile, but even they didn't deny that the miracles really happened. When Jesus raised Lazarus from the dead, for example, none of the chief priests or Pharisees disputed the miracle (John 11:45-48). Many hostile witnesses observed and scrutinized Christ's activities, so the Gospel writers would not have been able to fabricate the miracle stories.

Is some language in the Bible scientifically incorrect?

Some critics allege that the Bible is not scientifically accurate in view of its frequent use of phenomenological language—that is, the language of appearances. Ecclesiastes 1:5, for example, refers to the sun rising and setting. From a scientific perspective, the sun does not actually rise or set. But let's be fair. This is the same kind of language weather forecasters use today. "Rising" and "setting" are accepted ways of describing what the sun *appears* to be doing from an earthly perspective. The Bible's use of such language does not undermine its accuracy.

2

The Reliability of Scripture

Does good archaeological evidence support the Bible?

Yes! The Bible's accuracy and reliability have been proved and verified over and over again by archaeological finds produced by both believing and nonbelieving scholars. This includes verification for numerous customs, places, names, and events mentioned in the Bible.

Here's one example. For many years, historians questioned the existence of the Hittites (a powerful people who lived during the time of Abraham) because no archaeological digs had uncovered anything about them. Critics claimed the Hittites were pure myth. But in recent years, researchers have uncovered abundant archaeological evidence for the existence of the Hittites during the time of Abraham.

Today more than 25,000 archaeological discoveries verify biblical people, places, and events. And not one of these discoveries has contradicted or undermined anything found in the Bible!

Are the New Testament manuscripts trustworthy? What about all the variants the critics talk about?

We have more than 25,000 partial and complete manuscript copies of the New Testament. These manuscript copies are very ancient, and they are available for inspection. We also have some 36,000 quotations from the early church fathers and several thousand lectionaries (church-service books containing Scripture quotations used in the early centuries of Christianity). In fact, even if we did not have a single copy of the Bible, scholars could reconstruct all but 11 verses of the entire New Testament from quotations from the early church fathers. These quotes were written within 200 years of the time of Christ.

In the many thousands of manuscript copies we possess of the New Testament, scholars have discovered some 200,000 variants. This may seem like a staggering figure, but to those who study the issue, the numbers are not as serious as they may initially appear.

To begin, out of these 200,000 variants, 99.9 percent hold virtually no significance whatsoever. Many of these variants simply involve a missing letter in a word. Others involve reversing the order of two words (such as "Christ Jesus" instead of "Jesus Christ"). Sometimes one or more insignificant words are missing or a clarifying word is added.

Only about 40 of the variants have any real significance, and even those have no effect on any doctrine of the Christian faith or moral commandment. For more than 99 percent of the cases, the original text can be reconstructed to a practical certainty.

Are the Old Testament manuscripts trustworthy?

Yes! The Dead Sea Scrolls prove the accuracy of the

transmission of the Old Testament books of the Bible. These scrolls, discovered at Qumran in 1943, include Old Testament manuscripts written in 150 BC—more than a thousand years before the earliest Old Testament manuscripts previously in our possession. The two sets of manuscripts are essentially the same, with very few changes. (The entire book of Isaiah—66 chapters long—had only 13 changes.) The fact that the manuscripts are separated by a thousand years and are still essentially the same highlights how incredibly accurate they are.

Does the Bible indicate that God preserved Scripture through the ages?

Yes. The text of the Bible itself shows that God preserved the accuracy of biblical manuscripts. Jesus did not have the original autographs of the Old Testament writers; He had access only to copies. But He raised no doubts about the adequacy or accuracy of the Scriptures in His day, so we can safely assume that the first-century text of the Old Testament was a wholly adequate and accurate representation of the divine Word originally given. Jesus regarded the copies of His day as so close to the originals that He appealed to those copies as absolutely authoritative.

3

The Canon of Scripture

What is the canon of Scripture?

The English word *canon* comes from a Greek word that means "measuring stick." The word eventually came to be used metaphorically of books that were carefully scrutinized or "measured" and were recognized as being God's Word.

Were any New Testament books immediately recognized as belonging in the canon, or did that happen centuries later?

Many books written during New Testament times were immediately recognized as the Word of God. In 1 Timothy 5:18, the apostle Paul quoted an Old Testament reference and a New Testament reference and called them both (collectively) "Scripture" (Deuteronomy 25:4 and Luke 10:7). Only three years elapsed between the writing of the Gospel of Luke and the writing of 1 Timothy (about AD 60 and 63, respectively). Yet despite this, Paul (himself a Jew—a "Hebrew of Hebrews") does not hesitate to give Luke the same authority as the Old Testament book of Deuteronomy. For a New Testament book to be called Scripture so soon after it was written says volumes about Paul's view of the authority of New Testament books.

Further, the apostle Peter recognized the apostle Paul's writings as Scripture (2 Peter 3:16). And Paul himself understood that his own writings were inspired by God and therefore authoritative (1 Corinthians 14:37; 1 Thessalonians 2:13). Paul, of course, wrote about half of the books in the New Testament.

How did the early church recognize which books were canonical?

When the church formally recognized which books belonged in the canon, they applied five primary tests.

1. *Is the book written or backed by a prophet or apostle of God?* Church leaders reasoned that the Word of God, which is inspired by the Spirit of God for the people of God, must be communicated through a man of God (see Deuteronomy 18:18; 2 Peter 1:20-21).

2. *Is the book authoritative?* In other words, does this book ring with the sense of "Thus saith the Lord"?

3. *Does the book tell the truth about God as it is already known by previous revelation?* Agreement with all earlier revelation is essential (see Acts 17:11; Galatians 1:8).

4. *Does the book give evidence of having the power of God?* Any writing that does not exhibit

the transforming power of God in the lives
of its readers cannot have come from God
(2 Timothy 3:16-17; Hebrews 4:12).

5. *Was the book accepted by the people of God?* The
majority of God's people (not simply a faction)
will initially receive God's Word as such (see
Deuteronomy 31:24-26; Joshua 24:25-27;
Colossians 4:16; 1 Thessalonians 2:13; 5:27).

Why was the canonicity of certain New Testament books doubted for a while?

Hebrews was doubted because the author was
unknown. However, the book eventually came to be
viewed as having apostolic authority, if not apostolic
authorship.

James was doubted because of its apparent conflict
with Paul's teaching about salvation by faith alone. The
conflict was resolved by seeing the works James speaks of
as an outgrowth of real faith.

Second Peter was doubted because its style differs
from that of 1 Peter. However, Peter used a scribe to write
1 Peter (see 1 Peter 5:12), so a style conflict is not really a
problem.

Second and 3 John were doubted because the author
is called *elder*, not *apostle*. However, Peter (an apostle)
refers to himself as an elder (1 Peter 5:1). A person can be
both an elder and an apostle.

Jude was doubted because it refers to two noncanonical books—the Book of Enoch and the Assumption of Moses. This objection was eventually overcome because even Paul quoted from pagan poets (Acts 17:28; Titus 1:12).

The book of Revelation was doubted because it teaches a thousand-year reign of Christ. A local contemporary cult taught the same thing, so church leaders assumed Revelation must not be true Scripture. However, many of the earliest church fathers believed in a thousand-year reign of Christ too, so this objection was eventually seen as being without merit.

Does Mark 16:9-20 belong in the Bible?

Mark 16:9-20 is absent from two of the oldest Greek manuscripts in our possession—Codex Vaticanus and Codex Sinaiticus. As well, these verses are absent from the Old Latin Codex Bobbiensis, the Sinaitic Syriac manuscript, about 100 Armenian manuscripts, and the two oldest Georgian manuscripts. Further, Clement of Alexandria and Origen show no knowledge of the existence of these verses. Eusebius and Jerome attest that the passage was absent from almost all the Greek copies of Mark known to them. Understandably, then, many scholars believe that Mark 16:9-20 does not belong in the Bible. Fortunately, Mark 16:9-20 does not affect a single major doctrine of Christianity.

4

Interpreting Scripture

**Do Christians interpret the Bible
with wooden literalism?**

Evangelicals do not hold to a wooden literalism—
the kind that interprets biblical figures of speech literally.
What is understood to be symbolic and what is taken literally is based on the biblical context itself—such as when
Jesus used obviously figurative parables to communicate
spiritual truth.

A literal approach to Scripture recognizes that the
Bible contains a variety of literary genres, each of which
have certain peculiar characteristics that must be identified in order to interpret the text properly. Biblical genres
include history (Acts, for example), the dramatic epic
(Job), poetry (Psalms), wise sayings (Proverbs), apocalyp-
tic writings (Revelation), and more. An incorrect genre
judgment will lead one far astray in interpreting Scripture.

Even though the Bible contains a variety of literary
genres and many figures of speech, the biblical authors
most often employed literal statements to convey their
ideas. And where they use a literal means to express their
ideas, the Bible expositor must employ a corresponding
literal approach to explain these ideas. Without such a

method, communication between God and humankind is impossible.

What does "Scripture interprets Scripture" mean?

The entire body of holy Scripture is the guide for understanding the individual verses of Scripture. The interpretation of a specific passage must not contradict the total teaching of Scripture on a point. Individual verses exist not as isolated fragments but as parts of a whole. So, Scripture must interpret Scripture. If we would understand the parts, our wisest course is to get to know the whole.

How can we interpret the Old Testament?

Always interpret the Old Testament in view of the greater light of the New Testament. For example, Isaiah 6:1-5 tells us that Isaiah witnessed the incredible glory of God. The greater light of the New Testament, however, tells us that Isaiah actually saw Jesus' glory (John 12:41).

Likewise, the Exodus account tells us that God Almighty sustained His people in the wilderness sojourn (see Exodus 13:21-22; 14:15-22). But the greater light of the New Testament tells us that Christ was most definitely involved in sustaining His people in the wilderness (1 Corinthians 10:1-4).

By approaching the Old Testament through the greater light of the New Testament, we see things in the Old Testament we would not otherwise see.

Part 2

Common Questions About the Bible

5

The Old Testament

What is the gap theory of creation (Genesis 1:1-2)?

The gap theory teaches that there was an original creation (Genesis 1:1) and that as a result of Lucifer's rebellion and fall, the earth became chaos. The picture of formlessness, emptiness, and darkness in Genesis 1:2 is allegedly a picture of divine judgment, for God could not have originally created the earth this way. Millions of years are said to have taken place between verses 1 and 2.

This theory has a number of problems. For one thing, the grammar of Genesis 1:1-2 does not allow for a gap. Verse 1 is an independent clause; verse 2 is composed of three circumstantial clauses (explaining the condition of the earth when God began to create), and it is directly connected to verse 3. There is no break between verses

1 and 2. Grammatically, then, the gap theory just doesn't
fit.

The gap theory also assumes that the phrase *formless
and empty* means that creation was evil or that God had
judged it. However, its usage in Job 26:7 and Isaiah 45:18
does not support this idea.

Gap theorists also draw an artificial distinction
between the Hebrew verbs *bara* (which they define as "cre-
ating out of nothing"—Genesis 1:1) and *asa* (which they
define as "refashioning"—Genesis 1:7,16,25). A careful
study of these two verbs, however, reveals that they are
used interchangeably; *asa* does not mean "to refashion."
In view of these and other factors, I do not give much cre-
dence to the gap theory.

Are the days mentioned in Genesis 1:3–2:3 literal 24-hour days?

Theologians have debated this issue for centuries.
There are four primary views.

1. Some believe the days were *revelatory* days—
   that is, they were days during which God
   revealed the creation scene to Moses. (Exodus
   20:11, however, clearly contradicts this view.)

2. Others believe each day represents an age. Joel
   2:31 portrays a day as a long period of time.

3. Others believe the days are literal solar days,
   but each day was separated by a huge time-gap.

This allegedly accounts for the apparent long geological ages that science has discovered.

4. Still others believe the days are literal solar days with no time gap between them. This is my view.

In support of this latter view, the Genesis account refers to evening and morning, indicating literal days (Genesis 1:5). God created the sun to rule the day and the moon to rule the night, which indicates solar days (verse 16). Solar days also seem to be implied in Exodus 20:11, where we are told that "in six days the LORD made the heavens and the earth, the sea, and all that is in them, but he rested on the seventh day."

Moreover, Hebrew scholars tell us that without exceptions, whenever a number is used with the Hebrew word for day (*yom*), it refers to a literal solar day. Genesis says that God created the universe in six days, so it must be referring to literal solar days.

Genesis 2:17 indicates that Adam and Eve would die the day they ate the forbidden fruit. But they did not die, did they?

They *did* die—spiritually. The Hebrew word for death carries the idea of separation. Physical death involves the separation of the soul or spirit from the body. Spiritual death involves the separation of the human being from God. When Adam and Eve ate the forbidden fruit, they were immediately spiritually separated from God. (Their attempt to hide from God in the Garden of Eden indicates their awareness of this spiritual separation.) The moment of their sin, they became "dead in...transgressions and sins" (Ephesians 2:1). Their separation and isolation from God eventually led to their physical deaths.

Why did God accept Abel's offering but reject Cain's (Genesis 4:3-5)?

The answer has to do with the two men's differing attitudes. Abel gave not only the firstborn of his flock but even the choicest of the firstborn (Genesis 4:4). Abel gave the "best of the best" that was in his possession. Cain merely brought "some of the fruits of the soil" (verse 3). One gets the feeling that Cain routinely gathered some fruit and offered it to the Lord to fulfill his obligation.

Abel's faith was apparently another factor. In Hebrews 11:4 we read, "By faith Abel offered God a better sacrifice than Cain did. By faith he was commended as a righteous man, when God spoke well of his offerings." In contrast to Abel's faith and righteousness, Cain was apparently characterized by unbelief and unrighteousness.

Where did Cain get his wife (Genesis 4:17)?

Adam and Eve had a number of children. Genesis 5:4 says, "After Seth was born, Adam lived 800 years and had other sons and daughters." Adam and Eve were the first man and woman, and God had commanded them (and their descendants) to be fruitful and increase in number

(Genesis 1:28), so Cain probably married one of his many sisters, a niece, or even a grandniece.

In the early years of the human race, no genetic defects had yet developed as a result of the fall of man. By the time of Abraham, God had not yet declared this kind of marriage to be contrary to His will (see Genesis 20:12). Laws against incest apparently did not become enacted until the time of Moses (Leviticus 18:7-17; 20:11-12,14,17,20-21).

Are the sons of God mentioned in Genesis 6:2 evil angels?

This is a much-debated issue. A common view is that some evil angels cohabited with human women. Here are a few facts that support this view.

1. Some early Greek translations of the Hebrew Old Testament have the phrase "angels of God" instead of "sons of God." This reveals that some of the early Jews understood this phrase to be referring to angels.

2. The Hebrew phrase for "sons of God" (or more literally, "sons of *Elohim*") always refers to angels elsewhere in the Old Testament (see Job 1:6; 2:1; 38:7 NASB).

3. The "evil angel" interpretation of Genesis 6 may help explain why some angels are presently bound in prison and others are not (2 Peter 2:4).

Another view is that some fallen angels possessed human men who then cohabited with women. This view has the merit of providing a good explanation of how angels who are bodiless (Hebrews 1:14) and sexless (Matthew 22:30) could cohabit with humans.

Still another common interpretation is that the phrase "sons of God" refers to the godly line of Seth (the Redeemer's line—Genesis 4:25-26), who intermingled with the godless line of Cain. In support of this view is the fact that human beings are sometimes called sons (Isaiah 43:6). It is best not to be overly dogmatic over this disputed passage.

Does Genesis 6–9 depict a universal flood or a local flood?

It was apparently universal. The waters climbed so high on the earth that "all the high mountains under the entire heavens were covered" (Genesis 7:19). They rose so high that they "covered the mountains to a depth of more than twenty feet" (verse 20). The flood lasted 377 days (nearly 54 weeks), indicating more than just local flooding. Further, every living thing on the face of the earth perished (verses 22-23).

Why did God command Abraham to sacrifice his son as a burnt offering (Genesis 22:2)?

Genesis 22 indicates that God never intended Abraham to execute this command. God restrained Abraham's hand just in the nick of time (Genesis 22:10-12).

Common Questions About the Bible

Scholars agree that God was testing Abraham's faith. The test served to show that Abraham loved God more than he loved his own son.

Did God make the sun stand still in answer to Joshua's request (Joshua 10:12-14)?

Some scholars believe God may have slowed down or stopped the normal rotation of the earth so that Joshua's forces were able to complete their victory over the Amorites. Others suggest that God prolonged the daylight by some sort of unusual refraction of the sun's rays.

The Amorites worshipped the sun and the moon as deities. God brought about the defeat of the Amorites through the agency of their own gods. This showed the utter futility of their belief in false religion.

Did Jephthah sacrifice his daughter to God (Judges 11:30-39)?

Some scholars believe Jephthah actually did offer his own daughter as a burnt sacrifice to the Lord. But if he did, God certainly didn't endorse it. Jephthah was not under God's orders to do what he did. In fact, God had already forbidden human sacrifice (Leviticus 18:21; 20:2-5; Deuteronomy 12:31; 18:10).

The Bible recounts many things God doesn't agree with. God does not agree with the actions of Satan, but the Bible nevertheless accurately reports on them. In the present case, the author of Judges may have provided an objective account of the event without passing judgment.

Further, the book of Judges deals with a period in human history when everyone was doing what was right in his or her own eyes (see Judges 21:25 NASB). Jephthah may have simply done what was right in his own eyes, thereby victimizing his daughter. If Jephthah actually committed this act, we can only conclude that he was acting in great folly and was going against the will of God despite his apparent desire to please the Lord.

But this is not the only interpretation. Other scholars say Jephthah offered up his daughter in the sense of consecrating her for service at the tabernacle for the rest of her life and devoting her to celibacy. This would involve offering her spiritually instead of offering her physically as a burnt offering. As the apostle Paul said in Romans 12:1, we can offer our bodies to God as living sacrifices.

If Jephthah indeed offered his daughter as a living sacrifice, this necessarily would involve a life of perpetual virginity, which was a tremendous sacrifice in the Hebrew culture. She would not be able to bring up children to continue her father's lineage.

This may explain why his daughter responded by saying, "Grant me this one request...Give me two months to roam the hills and weep with my friends, because I will never marry" (Judges 11:37). She wept not because of an impending death but because she would never marry.

Did a witch at Endor actually summon the prophet Samuel from the dead (1 Samuel 28:3-25)?

Scholars have suggested several possible explanations.

Some believe the witch worked a miracle by demonic powers and actually brought Samuel back from the dead. In support of this view, certain Bible passages seem to indicate that demons have the power to perform lying signs and wonders (Matthew 7:22; 2 Corinthians 11:14; 2 Thessalonians 2:9-10; Revelation 16:14). This view is unlikely, however, because Scripture also reveals that death is final (Hebrews 9:27), the dead cannot return (2 Samuel 12:23; Luke 16:24-26), and demons cannot usurp or overpower God's authority over life and death (Job 1:10-12).

Others believe the witch did not actually bring up Samuel from the dead, but a demonic spirit simply impersonated the prophet. Those who hold to this view say that certain verses indicate that demons can deceive people who try to contact the dead (Leviticus 19:31; Deuteronomy 18:11; 1 Chronicles 10:13). This view is unlikely, however, because the passage seems to say that Samuel did in fact return from the dead, that he provided a prophecy that actually came to pass, and that demons would not have uttered God's truth because the devil is the father of lies (John 8:44).

Other scholars believe God sovereignly and miraculously allowed Samuel's spirit to appear in order to rebuke Saul for his sin. Samuel's spirit did not appear as a result of the woman's powers (for indeed, no human has this power—Luke 16:24-27; Hebrews 9:27) but because God sovereignly brought it about. This view is supported by the fact that Samuel actually seemed to return from the dead (1 Samuel 28:14), and this caused the witch to shriek with fear (see verse 12). That God allowed Samuel's spirit to appear on this one occasion should not be taken to mean that witches have any real power to summon the dead. God had a one-time purpose for this one-time special occasion.

Why did Solomon have so many wives (1 Kings 11:1-3)?

History reveals that Solomon was very aggressive in his foreign policy. To seal a treaty in ancient days, a lesser king often gave his daughter in marriage to the greater king (in this case, Solomon). Every time Solomon sealed a new treaty, he ended up with yet another wife. These wives were considered tokens of friendship and solidified the relationship between the two kings. Solomon may not have been personally acquainted with some of these wives even though he was married to them.

In this, Solomon was disobedient to the Lord. He was apparently so obsessed with power and wealth that his ambition overshadowed his spiritual life, and he fell into apostasy. He even worshipped some of the false gods of the women who married him. Moreover, by marrying more than one woman, Solomon disobeyed God's revealed will regarding monogamy. From the very beginning God created one woman for one man (see Genesis 1:27; 2:21-25; Deuteronomy 17:17).

6

The New Testament

Why did God reveal Christ's birth to astrologers—the Magi (Matthew 2:1-2)?

The Magi were not occultic seers and sorcerers in the sense that today's astrologers are. They were basically experts in the study of the stars. We might loosely equate them today to specialists in astronomy. Tradition tells us that there were three Magi who visited Christ, and they are said to be kings. But we do not know this for certain.

Did Jesus heal one blind man or two at Jericho, and was He entering or leaving the city (Matthew 20:29-34; Mark 10:46-52; Luke 18:35-43)?

Jesus may have been leaving old Jericho and nearing new Jericho (there were two Jerichos in those days). If He was at a place between the two Jerichos, then depending on one's perspective, He could be viewed as leaving one Jericho or entering the other Jericho.

Apparently, two blind men needed healing, but Bartimaeus was the more aggressive of the two, so Mark and Luke mention only him. Another possible explanation is that the blind men pled with Jesus as He entered either the old or new Jericho, but they did not receive their actual healings until Jesus was leaving Jericho. Or perhaps Jesus healed one blind man as He was entering Jericho and healed two other blind men as he was leaving Jericho. Though we can't know for sure how the miracle happened, we can reconcile the Gospel accounts in several ways.

Did Judas die by hanging or by falling onto some rocks (Matthew 27:5; Acts 1:18)?

Matthew 27:5 tells us that Judas died by hanging himself. Acts 1:18 tells us that Judas fell onto some rocks and his body burst open. Both accounts are true. Apparently Judas first hanged himself. Then, at some point, the rope either broke or loosened so that his body slipped from it and fell to the rocks below and burst open. Neither account alone is complete. Taken together, we have a full picture of what happened to Judas.

Are we to hate our family for Jesus' sake (Luke 14:26)?

In the Hebrew mind-set, to hate simply meant to love less. Jesus was thus communicating that our supreme love must be for Him alone. Everything and everyone else must take second place. This is in keeping with what Jesus said in Matthew 10:37: "Anyone who loves his father or mother more than me is not worthy of me." Measuring our supreme love for Christ against all other lesser loves may make these lesser loves seem like hate by comparison.

Are we to do greater miracles than Jesus did (John 14:12)?

In this verse Jesus was saying that His many followers would do things greater in *extent* (all over the world) and greater in *effect* (multitudes being touched by the power of God). Jesus was referring to the whole scope of the impact of God's people and the church on the entire world throughout all history. In other words, He was speaking quantitatively, not qualitatively.

Part 3

God

7

The Triune God

The word *Trinity* is not in the Bible. Is the doctrine unbiblical?

Though the word *Trinity* is not mentioned in the Bible, the concept is clearly derived from its pages. Jehovah's Witnesses say the doctrine of the Trinity is unbiblical because the word is not in the Bible. But the word *Jehovah* does not appear in the Bible either. (*Jehovah* was originally formed by superstitious Jewish scribes who joined the consonants of two biblical words: *YHWH* and *Adonai*. The result was *Yahowah*, or *Jehovah*. They did this to avoid breaking the third of the Ten Commandments, which prohibits misusing God's name.) If you reject the doctrine of the Trinity because the word *Trinity* does not appear in the Bible, the doctrine of Jehovah must also be false because this term does not appear in the Bible either. The more appropriate question is this: Is the doctrine taught in the Bible?

Does the Bible support the doctrine of the Trinity?

Yes. The doctrine of the Trinity is based on three lines of evidence: (1) There is only one true God, (2) there are three persons who are God, and (3) *three-in-oneness* exists within the Godhead.

Before we examine these lines of evidence, let's clarify what we *do not* mean by the word *Trinity*. We must avoid two errors.

1. Tritheism is the belief that the Godhead is composed of three utterly distinct individuals.

2. Modalism is the belief that the Godhead is one person only and the triune aspect of His being is no more than three fields of interest, activities, and manifestations.

The fallacy of these errors will become clearer as we examine the biblical evidence for the Trinity below.

There is one God. The fact that there is only one true God is the consistent testimony of Scripture from Genesis to Revelation. It is like a thread that runs through every page of the Bible. God positively affirmed through Isaiah the prophet, "I am the first and I am the last; apart from me there is no God" (Isaiah 44:6; see also 46:9; John 5:44; 17:3; Romans 3:29-30; 16:27; 1 Corinthians 8:4; Galatians 3:20; Ephesians 4:6; 1 Timothy 2:5; James 2:19).

There are three persons who are called God. The Father is God (1 Peter 1:2); Jesus is God (John 20:28; Hebrews

1:8); and the Holy Spirit is God (Acts 5:3-4). Moreover, each of the three persons on different occasions are seen to possess the attributes of deity, including omnipresence (Acts 17:27; Matthew 28:20; Psalm 139:7), omniscience (Romans 11:33-34; Matthew 9:4; 1 Corinthians 2:10), omnipotence (1 Peter 1:5; Matthew 28:18; Romans 15:19), and holiness (Revelation 15:4; Acts 3:14; John 16:7-14).

There is three-in-oneness in the Godhead. We read in Matthew 28:19: "Go therefore and make disciples of all nations, baptizing them in the name of the Father and the Son and the Holy Spirit." The word *name* is singular in the Greek, indicating that there is one God, but there are three distinct persons within the Godhead—the Father, the Son, and the Holy Spirit.

How can three "persons" be in one God?

Most theologians acknowledge that the term *person* is an imperfect expression of what the Bible communicates. Some believe the word distracts from the unity of the Trinity. Certainly, God is not three separate individuals, such as Peter, John, and Matthew, who have different characteristics. Rather, the Godhead includes three personal self-distinctions—each with mind, emotions, and will, and each individually engaging in I-Thou relationships with the others. Each of the three is aware of the others, speaks to the others, and carries on a loving relationship with the others. *Person* is thus the best word we have.

8

Errors About the Doctrine of God

Is *Jehovah* God's true name?

This name is not found in the Hebrew and Greek Bible manuscripts. The Old Testament contains the name *Yahweh*—or, more literally, *YHWH* (Old Testament Hebrew had only consonants).

Regarding the term *Jehovah*, ancient Jews had a superstitious dread of pronouncing the name *YHWH*. They felt that if they uttered this name, they might violate the third commandment, which deals with misusing God's name (Exodus 20:7). To avoid the possibility of breaking this commandment, the Jews for centuries substituted the name *Adonai* (Lord) or some other name in its place whenever they came across it in public readings of Scripture. Eventually, the fearful Hebrew scribes decided to form a new word (*Jehovah*) by combining the vowels from *Adonai* and the consonants *YHWH*.

Thus, there is no biblical justification for the term *Jehovah*. Scholars are not precisely clear how to pronounce the Hebrew word *YHWH*. Though most modern scholars believe *Yahweh* is the correct rendering (as I do), we cannot be sure about that. Perhaps this is one reason why some legitimate translations—such as the American

Standard Version of 1901—used the term *Jehovah*. Most modern translations use the word LORD (with small caps) to render the term *YHWH*.

Why did God, who is all-powerful, have to rest after six days of creation (Genesis 2:2)?

God did not have to rest in the sense that His physical energy had become depleted and He needed to recuperate. Rather, the Hebrew word for rest means "cease from activity." Genesis 2:2 simply affirms that God completed His work of creation and then stopped. There was nothing further to do.

Is God a wrathful judge in the Old Testament and a loving Father in the New Testament?

Both the Old and New Testaments point to one and the same God—and this God loves *and* judges. On the one hand, God judged people in Old Testament times when the circumstances called for it. This was the case when He sent ten horrible plagues against the Egyptians (Exodus 7–11). But He also displayed love and grace throughout the Old Testament. When Adam and Eve sinned, God promised a Redeemer—an act of love and grace (Genesis 3:15). God's provision of an ark for Noah and his family was another act of love and grace (Genesis 6:9-22).

In the New Testament, God continually manifested His love through the person of Jesus Christ—He was love incarnate. But some of God's most scathing denouncements—especially in regard to the Jewish leaders—came from the mouth of Jesus (see Matthew 23:27-28,33).

The God of the Old and New Testaments is a God of love *and* judgment.

Does Genesis 1:26-27 teach that there is more than one God?

No. The word used of God in Genesis 1:26-27, *Elohim*, does have a plural ending (*-im*). But this is called a "plural of majesty," pointing to the majesty, dignity, and greatness of the one true God. The plural ending gives a fuller, more majestic sense to God's name.

The plural pronouns in Genesis 1 ("Let *us* make man in *our* image") are grammatical necessities. The plural pronoun *us*, for example, is required by the plural ending of *Elohim*. One demands the other. This passage speaks of only one God.

Is Christianity sexist when presenting God as a Father?

God values both men and women equally. God created both men and women in His image (Genesis 1:26). Christian men and women are positionally equal before God (Galatians 3:28). The four Gospels indicate that Jesus exalted women in a patriarchal Jewish culture (see John 4). So Christianity is not sexist. Rather, Jesus, the head of Christianity, countered the sexism of His day.

God is not a gender being as humans are. He is not male. God is called a Father because He is personal. Unlike the dead and impersonal idols of paganism, the true God is a personal being who relates to us. In fact, we can even call Him *Abba*, which loosely means "Daddy." That depicts the intimacy of the relationship we can have with Him.

Moses spoke to God "face to face" (Exodus 33:11). Does that mean God has a physical body?

No. Scripture informs us that God is spirit (John 4:24), and a spirit does not have flesh and bones (Luke 24:39). The description of Moses speaking to God "face to face" cannot be taken to mean that God actually has a physical face. Rather, the phrase is simply a Hebrew way of indicating that they spoke personally, directly, and intimately. Moses was in the direct presence of God and interacted with Him on a personal and intimate basis.

Human beings are created in God's image (Genesis 1:26-27). Does that mean God has a physical body?

Genesis 1:26-27 does not teach that man is created in the *physical* image of God. God is spirit (John 4:24), and a spirit does not have flesh and bones (Luke 24:39). In fact, God is invisible (John 1:18; Colossians 1:15; 1 Timothy 1:17).

Human beings are created in God's image because they share, though imperfectly and finitely, God's communicable attributes such as life, personality, truth, wisdom, love, holiness, and justice. Because we are created in God's image, we can have spiritual fellowship with Him.

9

God the Holy Spirit

The Holy Spirit is unnamed. Does that mean the Spirit is not a person?

No. Spiritual beings are not always named in Scripture. For example, evil spirits are rarely named in Scripture. Instead, they are identified by their character (unclean, wicked, and so forth—see Matthew 12:45). The Holy Spirit is identified by His primary character, which is holiness.

The Holy Spirit is in fact related to the name of the other persons of the Trinity in Matthew 28:19: "Therefore go and make disciples of all nations, baptizing them in the name of the Father and of the Son and of the Holy Spirit." Just as the Father and the Son are persons, so the Holy Spirit is a person.

The Holy Spirit fills many people at the same time (Acts 2:4). Is He therefore a force and not a person?

Ephesians 3:19 speaks of God filling all the Ephesian believers. Likewise, Ephesians 4:10 speaks of Christ filling the whole universe, and Ephesians 1:23 speaks of Christ as the one who "fills everything in every way." The fact that

God and Christ can fill all things does not mean that the Father and Jesus are not persons. In the same way, the fact that the Holy Spirit can fill numerous people does not mean He is not a person.

Does the Bible teach that the Holy Spirit is a person?

The three primary attributes of personality are mind, emotions, and will. The Holy Spirit's mind is evident in 1 Corinthians 2:10, where we are told that "the Spirit searches all things." Verse 11 indicates that the Holy Spirit knows the thoughts of God. Romans 8:27 refers to "the mind of the Spirit." (See also Isaiah 11:2; Ephesians 1:17.)

The Holy Spirit's emotions are evident in Ephesians 4:30, where we are admonished, "Do not grieve the Holy Spirit of God." The Holy Spirit feels the emotion of grief when believers sin (Ephesians 4:25-29).

The Holy Spirit's will is evident in 1 Corinthians 12:11, where we are told that the Holy Spirit distributes spiritual gifts "to each one, just as He determines." The phrase "He determines" translates the Greek word *bouletai*, which refers to "decisions of the will after previous deliberation."

Besides having these attributes of personality, the Holy Spirit does many things that only a person can do. For example, the Holy Spirit teaches believers (John 14:26), testifies (John 15:26), guides (Romans 8:14), commissions people to service (Acts 13:1-4), and issues commands to believers (Acts 8:29).

Is the baptism of the Holy Spirit the same thing as the filling of the Holy Spirit?

No. These are two separate ministries of the Holy Spirit. Baptism is a one-time event that takes place at the moment of conversion (1 Corinthians 12:13). The baptism of the Holy Spirit joins a believer to the body of Christ. If baptism did not happen at the moment of conversion, some believers would be saved but would not belong to the body of Christ, which of course is not possible.

By contrast, the filling of the Holy Spirit is not a one-time event. In fact, God desires that the filling be a continual and ongoing experience for us. In Ephesians 5:18 we are instructed, "Do not get drunk on wine, which leads to debauchery. Instead, be filled with the Spirit."

The word *filled* in this verse is a present tense imperative in the Greek. The present tense means that it should be a perpetual, ongoing experience. The imperative means it is a command from God. Being filled with the Spirit is not a mere option but rather a divine imperative for Christians.

To be filled with the Spirit is to be controlled by the Spirit. Instead of being controlled by wine and the things of this world, we are to be under the control of the Spirit.

What does the Bible say about speaking in tongues? Is this a spiritual gift I should be seeking?

The Holy Spirit is the one who bestows spiritual gifts on believers (1 Corinthians 12:11). Not every Christian has every gift. So I think Christians should be happy with whatever gift the Holy Spirit has sovereignly decided to give them. Here are four scriptural facts about speaking in tongues.

1. Speaking in tongues is not an evidence of the baptism of the Holy Spirit. Not all the Corinthians spoke in tongues (1 Corinthians 14:5), but they had all been baptized (12:13).

2. The fruit of the Holy Spirit (Galatians 5:22-23) does not include speaking in tongues. Therefore, Christlikeness does not require speaking in tongues.

3. Most of the New Testament writers are silent on tongues. Only three books (Mark, Acts, and 1 Corinthians) mention it (and Mark 16:17 is not in the two best Greek manuscripts). Significantly, many of the other New Testament books speak a great deal about the Holy Spirit but don't mention speaking in tongues.

4. Other gifts are more important gifts than tongues, and these are to be sought (1 Corinthians 12:28,31).

What is the sin against the Holy Spirit (Matthew 12:31-32)?

Matthew 12:31-32 says, "Every sin and blasphemy will be forgiven men, but the blasphemy against the Spirit will

not be forgiven...Anyone who speaks against the Holy
Spirit will not be forgiven, either in this age or in the age
to come."

The backdrop to this passage is that the Jewish leaders, who had just witnessed a mighty miracle of Christ,
should have recognized that Jesus performed this miracle in the power of the Holy Spirit. After all, the Hebrew
Scriptures, of which the Jewish leaders were well familiar,
prophesied that when the Messiah came He would perform many mighty miracles in the power of the Spirit (for
example, see Isaiah 35:5-6). Instead, these Jewish leaders claimed that Christ did this and other miracles in the
power of the devil, the *unholy* spirit. This was a sin against
the Holy Spirit. This shows that these Jewish leaders had
hardened themselves against the things of God.

Matthew 12 describes a unique situation among the
Jewish leaders, and the actual committing of this sin
requires the presence of the Messiah on earth doing His
messianic miracles. In view of this, I do not think this sin
can be reduplicated exactly today as described in Matthew 12.

People can repent of their personal sins (whatever they
be) and turn to God as long as they have breath. Until the
moment of death, every human being has the opportunity to turn to God and receive the free gift of salvation
(Ephesians 2:8-9).

Part 4

Jesus Christ

10

The Incarnation of Jesus Christ

**Why do the Gospels include two different genealo-
gies of Christ (Matthew 1:1-17; Luke 3:23-38)?**

Up to David, the two genealogies are practically the
same. In fact, they share 18 or 19 names, depending on
whether Matthan and Matthat are the same person. From
David on, they are very different. Only two of the names
from David to Joseph coincide—Shealtiel and Zerubba-
bel. Why are they different?

Matthew's genealogy traces Joseph's ancestors and documents Jesus' inheritance of the legal title to the throne
of David. As Joseph's adopted Son, Jesus became his legal
heir so far as his inheritance was concerned. The "of whom
was born Jesus" (Matthew 1:16) is a feminine relative pronoun, clearly indicating that Jesus was the physical child of
Mary and that Joseph was not His physical father.

Matthew traced the line from Abraham through
David to Joseph in 41 links. Matthew obviously did not

list every individual in the genealogy. Jewish reckoning
did not require every name in order to satisfy a genealogy.

God gave Abraham and David the two unconditional
covenants pertaining to the Messiah. Matthew's Gospel
was written to Jews, so Matthew wanted to prove to Jews
that Jesus was the promised Messiah. This would demand
a fulfillment of the Abrahamic covenant (Genesis 12) and
the Davidic covenant (2 Samuel 7). Matthew was calling
attention to the fact that Jesus came to fulfill the covenants
made with Israel's forefathers.

Luke's genealogy, by contrast, traces Mary's lineage
and carries all the way back beyond the time of Abraham to Adam and the commencement of the human
race. Matthew's genealogy points to Jesus as the Jewish
Messiah, but Luke's genealogy points to Jesus as the Son
of Man, Jesus' favorite title for Himself in Luke's Gospel.
Matthew's genealogy shows the Messiah's relationship to
the Jews, but Luke's genealogy shows the Messiah's relationship to the entire human race.

Did Jesus, who is eternal God, become fully man?

Yes. To deny either the undiminished deity or the perfect humanity of Christ is to put oneself outside the pale
of orthodoxy (see 1 John 4:2-3). Innumerable passages in
the New Testament confirm Christ's full humanity. For
example, Hebrews 2:14 tells us that "since the children
have flesh and blood, [Jesus] shared in their humanity
so that by his death he might destroy him who holds

the power of death—that is, the devil." Romans 8:3 says that God sent Jesus "in the likeness of sinful man to be a sin offering." The apostle Paul affirms that "in Christ all the fullness of the Deity lives in bodily form" (Colossians 2:9).

Though Jesus never surrendered any aspect of His deity in the Incarnation, He experienced normal human development through infancy, childhood, adolescence, and into adulthood. According to Luke 2:40, Jesus grew, became strong, and was filled with wisdom. These things could be said only of His humanity, not His divine nature.

Likewise, Luke 2:52 tells us that "Jesus grew in wisdom and stature, and in favor with God and men." This too can be said only of His humanity.

Christ's development as a human being was normal in every respect except for two: Christ always did the will of God, and He never sinned (see Hebrews 4:15; 7:26).

Why was the virgin birth necessary?

The virgin birth was necessary for five reasons:

1. Without the virgin birth, Jesus would have been merely a natural being.

2. The virgin birth prevented Jesus from inheriting a sin nature from Joseph (see 2 Corinthians 5:21; Hebrews 4:15; 7:26; 1 Peter 2:22-24).

3. The Old Testament reveals that Jesus had to be both God and man as the Messiah (see Isaiah

7:14; 9:6). This could only be fulfilled through the virgin birth.

4. Jesus is our Kinsman-Redeemer. In Old Testament times, the next of kin (one related by blood) always functioned as the kinsman-redeemer of a family member who needed redemption from jail. Jesus became related to us by blood so He could function as our Kinsman-Redeemer and rescue us from sin. This required the virgin birth.

5. The virgin birth was necessary because Jesus was predicted to come from the seed of the woman (Genesis 3:15 NASB).

Did Christ give up any of His divine attributes in the Incarnation?

Christ did not give up any attributes. So what does Paul mean when he writes that Christ "made himself nothing" (Philippians 2:6-8)?

First, Christ veiled the glory that was His for all eternity as God. This was necessary in order for Him to take on the appearance of a man. Christ never surrendered His glory (recall the glory He displayed on the Mount of Transfiguration in Matthew 17). Rather, Jesus veiled His glory in order to dwell among mortal human beings (see Isaiah 6:5; John 12:41; Revelation 1:17).

Second, Christ "made himself nothing" by voluntarily

not using some of His divine attributes on some occasions so He could accomplish His objectives. Christ could never have actually surrendered any of His attributes, for then He would have ceased to be God. But He voluntarily chose not to use some of them on some occasions during His time on earth in order to live among human beings and their limitations (see Matthew 24:36, for example).

Third and most important, Christ "made himself nothing" by taking on the appearance of a man and the very nature of a servant. Christ was thus truly human. This humanity was subject to temptation, distress, weakness, pain, sorrow, and limitation.

How can two natures—a divine nature and a human nature—be united in Jesus?

To answer this, we must first understand what a nature is. The word *nature*, when used of Christ's divinity, refers to all that belongs to deity, including all the attributes of deity. When used of Christ's humanity, *nature* refers to all that belongs to humanity, including all the attributes of humanity.

Though Jesus in the Incarnation had both a human and a divine nature, He was only one person—as indicated by His consistent use of *I*, *me*, and *mine* in reference to Himself. Jesus never used the words *us*, *we*, or *ours* in reference to His human-divine person.

Scripture reveals that the attributes of one nature are never attributed to the other, but the attributes of both

natures are properly attributed to Christ's one person.
Thus He had what seem to be contradictory qualities at
the same time. He was finite and yet infinite, weak and
yet omnipotent, increasing in knowledge and yet omniscient, limited to being in one place at one time and yet
omnipresent. In the Incarnation, the person of Christ is
the partaker of the attributes of both natures, so that whatever may be affirmed of either nature—human or divine—
may be affirmed of the one person.

Christ in His human nature knew hunger (Luke 4:2),
weariness (John 4:6), and the need for sleep (Luke 8:23).
Christ in His divine nature was omniscient (John 2:24),
omnipresent (John 1:48), and omnipotent (John 11).

Could Christ have sinned during His earthly ministry?

I do not believe so. This view, known as the impecca-
bility of Christ, is based on these points:

1. In His divine nature, He is immutable and does
   not change.

2. In His divine nature, He is omniscient,
   knowing all the consequences of sin.

3. In His divine nature, He is omnipotent in His
   ability to resist sin.

4. Hebrews 4 tells us that He was tempted yet was
   without sin.

5. Christ did not have the sin nature all other

human beings have, and He was perfectly holy
from birth (Luke 1:35).

6. There is an analogy between the written Word
of God (the Bible) and the living Word of God
(Christ). Just as the Bible has a human element
and a divine element and is completely without
error, so Christ is fully divine and fully human
and is completely without (and unable to) sin.

This does not mean Christ's temptations were unreal.
Christ was genuinely tempted (Hebrews 2:18), but the
temptations stood no chance of luring Christ to sin. It is
much like a canoe trying to attack a U.S. battleship. The
attack is genuine, but it stands no chance of success.

11

Is Jesus Lesser than the Father?

In Mark 10:17-18, did Jesus imply that He is not good?

In Mark 10:17-18 a young ruler referred to Jesus as
"good teacher." Jesus responded, "Why do you call me
good?...No one is good—except God alone."

Jesus was not claiming He was not good or denying
He was God. Rather, He was asking the man to examine

the implications of what he was saying. In effect, Jesus said, "Do you realize what you are saying when you call Me good? Are you rightly recognizing that I am God?" Jesus' words were thus a veiled claim to deity.

Jesus didn't know the day or hour of His return. Does this mean He is less than God (Mark 13:32)?

No. But explaining this issue requires a little theological background. Prior to the Incarnation, the eternal Son of God was one person with one nature—a divine nature. In the Incarnation, He had two natures (divine and human) while remaining one person.

Thus Christ at the same moment in time had what seem to be contradictory qualities. He was finite and yet infinite, weak and yet omnipotent, increasing in knowledge and yet omniscient, limited to being in one place at one time and yet omnipresent. Only from Christ's humanity could He say that He did not know the day or hour of His return. If Jesus had been speaking from the perspective of His divinity, He would not have said the same thing.

Scripture is clear that in His divine nature, Jesus is omniscient. The apostle John said that Jesus "did not need man's testimony about man, for he knew what was in a man" (John 2:25). Jesus' disciples said, "Now we can see that you know all things" (John 16:30). After the resurrection, when Jesus asked Peter for the third time if Peter loved Him, Peter responded, "Lord, you know all things;

you know that I love you" (John 21:17). Jesus knew just where the fish were in the water (Luke 5:4-6; John 21:6-11), and He knew just which fish contained the coin (Matthew 17:27). He knew the Father as the Father knew Him (Matthew 11:27; John 7:29; 8:55; 10:15; 17:25).

How can Jesus be God's only begotten Son (John 3:16 NASB) and God at the same time?

The words *only begotten* do not mean that Christ was created (as the ancient heretic Arius taught). Rather, they mean He was unique, or one of a kind. Jesus is the Son of God in the sense that He has the same nature as the Father—a divine nature. Whenever Christ claimed to be the Son of God, His Jewish critics tried to stone Him because they correctly understood Him as claiming to be God (see John 5:18).

How is the Father greater than Christ (John 14:28)?

Jesus is not speaking in this verse about His nature or His essential being. He had earlier said, "I and the Father are one" (John 10:30). Rather, Jesus is speaking of His lowly position in the Incarnation. The Father was seated on the throne of highest majesty in heaven, but His incarnate Son was despised and rejected of men, surrounded by implacable enemies, and soon to be nailed to a criminal's cross.

In what sense is God the head of Christ?

In 1 Corinthians 11:3 we read that "the head of Christ

is God." We also read that "the head of the woman is man." Of course, men and women are utterly equal in their essential nature. Both are human, and both are created in God's image (Genesis 1:26-28), and they are one in Christ (Galatians 3:28). This shows that men and women are completely equal in terms of their nature even though an authority structure exists between them in the family and in the church.

Likewise, Christ and the Father are equal in their divine being (Jesus said "I and the Father are one"—John 10:30) even though Jesus is under the Father's authority. The persons in the Godhead are equal in being yet have an authority structure.

Jesus is called the firstborn (Colossians 1:15). Does that mean He is a created being?

No. The word *firstborn* does not mean "first-created." Rather, the word (Greek: *prototokos*) means "first in rank, preeminent one, heir." The word describes Christ's positional preeminence and supremacy. He is the firstborn of creation in the sense that He is positionally preeminent over creation and is supreme over all things. This makes sense, for Christ is also the Creator of all things (Colossians 1:16).

Was Jesus just a good moral teacher?

No moral teacher would claim that the destiny of the world rests in his hands or that people would spend eternity in heaven or hell depending on whether they believed in him, but Jesus did (John 6:26-40). And for Jesus to convince people that He was God (John 8:58) and the Savior of the world (Luke 19:10) when He really was not would be immoral. So to say that Jesus was just a good moral teacher and nothing more makes virtually no sense.

12

The Deity of Christ

Are Jesus and Yahweh the same?

A comparison of the Old and New Testaments provides powerful testimony to Jesus' identity as Yahweh. In Zechariah 12:10, for example, Yahweh says, "They will look on me, the one they have pierced." Yahweh is obviously referring to the crucifixion (see Revelation 1:7).

New Testament writers applied Old Testament passages about Yahweh to Jesus. For instance, Isaiah 40:3 says, "In the desert prepare the way for the LORD [Yahweh]; make straight in the wilderness a highway for our God [*Elohim*]." Mark's Gospel tells us that Isaiah's words were fulfilled in the ministry of John the Baptist preparing the way for Jesus Christ (Mark 1:2-4).

Many of Yahweh's actions in the Old Testament are performed by Christ in the New Testament. For example, in Psalm 119 we are told about a dozen times that Yahweh is the one who gives and preserves life. In the New Testament, Jesus claims this power for Himself (John 5:21).

Did Jesus become the Son of God, or is He eternally the Son of God?

Jesus is eternally the Son of God. Though the term *Son of* can refer to "offspring of," it also means "of the order of." The phrase is often used this way in the Old Testament. For example, *sons of the prophets* meant "of the order of prophets" (1 Kings 20:35). *Sons of the singers* meant "of the order of singers" (Nehemiah 12:28 NASB). Likewise, the phrase *Son of God* means "of the order of God" and is a claim to undiminished deity (see John 5:18; 19:7).

Scripture portrays Christ as the Son of God before His birth in Bethlehem. For example, we read that God sent His Son into the world (John 3:16-17), implying that Jesus was the Son of God before the Incarnation. Further, Hebrews 1:2 says God created the universe through His Son, implying that Christ was the Son of God prior to the Creation.

Why did Jesus often say "I tell you" instead of "declares the LORD" as the Old Testament prophets often did?

Jesus' teachings were ultimate and final. He never wavered in this. He unflinchingly placed His teachings above those of Moses and the prophets—and in a Jewish culture at that! He always spoke in His own authority.

He never retracted anything He said, never guessed or spoke with uncertainty, never made revisions, never contradicted Himself, and never apologized for what He said. He even asserted, "Heaven and earth will pass away, but my words will never pass away" (Mark 13:31), elevating His words to the realm of heaven.

One cannot read the Gospels long before recognizing that Jesus regarded Himself and His message as inseparable. Jesus' teachings have ultimate authority because He is God. The words of Jesus are the very words of God!

Some cultists say we should not worship Jesus. What do the Scriptures say about this?

Jesus Christ was worshipped (Greek: *proskuneo*) as God many times according to the Gospel accounts, and He always accepted such worship as perfectly appropriate. Jesus accepted worship from Thomas (John 20:28), the angels (Hebrews 1:6), some wise men (Matthew 2:11), a leper (Matthew 8:2), a ruler (Matthew 9:18), a blind man (John 9:38), a Canaanite woman (Matthew 15:25), Mary Magdalene (Matthew 28:9), and the disciples (Matthew 28:17). All these verses contain the word *proskuneo*, the same word used of worshipping the Father in the New Testament.

Jesus never sought to correct His followers when they bowed down and worshipped Him. The fact that Jesus willingly received and condoned worship on various occasions says a lot about His true identity, for Scripture consistently commands people to worship God alone (Exodus 34:14).

Is Jesus Himself also God the Father and the Holy Spirit?

Scripture is clear that there is one God, but the Father, Son, and Holy Spirit are distinct persons within the Godhead. Scripture tells us that the Father sent the Son (John 3:16-17), the Father and Son love each other (John 3:35), and the Father and Son speak to each other (John 11:41-42). Moreover, the Father knows the Son and the Son knows the Father (Matthew 11:27), and Jesus is our advocate with the Father (1 John 2:1).

Jesus clearly is not the Holy Spirit, for the Holy Spirit descended onto Jesus at His baptism (Luke 3:22). Jesus calls the Holy Spirit "another Counselor" (John 14:16). Jesus sent the Holy Spirit (John 15:26), and the Holy Spirit glorifies Jesus (John 16:13-14).

13

Christ in the Old Testament

Was Melchizedek a preincarnate appearance of Christ in the Old Testament?

I do not think so. Hebrews 7:3 says Melchizedek is *like* the Son of God; it doesn't say he is the Son of God Himself. It seems best to view Melchizedek as an actual historical person—a mere human being—who was a *type* of Christ. (A type is someone or something that prophetically foreshadows someone or something else.)

Hebrews 7:3 also says Melchizedek is "without father or mother, without genealogy, without beginning of days or end of life." This may sound as if he is Christ Himself. However, many scholars argue that this verse simply means that the Old Testament has no record of these events. To emphasize Melchizedek's role as a type, Scripture purposely omits all mention of his birth, parentage, or ancestors. This is not to deny that Melchizedek had a father or mother. Rather, such information was purposefully omitted in Genesis 14 so that Melchizedek might typologically point to the Messiah, the *Antitype*.

Melchizedek's name combines two words meaning "king" and "righteous." He was also a priest, so he foreshadows Christ as a righteous king-priest. Melchizedek was also the king of Salem (which means peace). This points forward to Christ as the King of peace.

What is a theophany?

The word *theophany* comes from two Greek words: *theos* (God) and *phaino* (to appear). A theophany is an appearance or manifestation of God, usually in visible, bodily form. I believe that theophanies in the Old Testament were actually preincarnate appearances of Christ. The principal theophany of the Old Testament is the Angel of the Lord (or, more literally, Angel of Yahweh).

Were Old Testament appearances of the Angel of the Lord actually preincarnate appearances of Christ?

Yes, I believe so. Three primary lines of evidence support this view.

The Angel of the Lord is God. In the Old Testament, the Angel of the Lord (or Angel of Yahweh) makes definite claims to deity. In the account of the burning bush, the Angel of Yahweh identified Himself to Moses as "the God of your father, the God of Abraham, the God of Isaac and the God of Jacob" (Exodus 3:6).

The Angel of Yahweh is distinct from Yahweh. Though the Angel of Yahweh was recognized as Yahweh, He is also recognized as distinct from Yahweh. In Zechariah 1:12, for example, the Angel of Yahweh intercedes to another person called Yahweh on behalf of the people of Jerusalem and Judah.

The Angel of the Lord must be the preincarnate Christ. This inference is based on three lines of evidence:

First, Christ is the visible God of the New Testament, and neither the Father (John 5:37; Colossians 1:15; 1 Timothy 1:17; 6:16) nor the Holy Spirit (John 14:17) characteristically manifest themselves visibly. This implies that Christ was the one who visibly appeared in Old Testament times as the Angel of Yahweh.

Second, just as Christ was sent by the Father in the New Testament (John 3:17), so the Angel of Yahweh was sent by Yahweh in the Old Testament (Judges 13:8-9). The divine pattern in Scripture is that the Father sends the Son.

Third, the divine Angel and Christ engaged in amazingly similar ministries. For example, besides interceding for the people of God (Zechariah 1:12-13; 3:1-2; John 17; Romans 8:34; Hebrews 7:25), both the Angel and Christ commissioned individuals for service (Exodus 3:7-8; Judges 6:11-23; 13:1-21; Matthew 4:18-20; 28:19-20; Acts 26:14-18) and rescued slaves (Exodus 3; Galatians 1:4; 1 Thessalonians 1:10; 2 Timothy 4:18; Hebrews 2:14-15).

It is critical to anchor in our minds the precise sense in which Jesus can properly be called an Angel. In accordance with its Hebrew root, the word *Angel* was used of Christ because He is a messenger, one who is sent, an envoy. This usage of the word indicates that Christ was acting on behalf of the Father. Christ, as the Angel of Yahweh, was a divine intermediary between God the Father and man.

14

The Resurrection

How important is the resurrection?

Very important! The apostle Paul said, "If Christ has not been raised, our preaching is useless and so is your faith" (1 Corinthians 15:14). If the resurrection did not really happen, the apostles were false witnesses, our faith is futile, we are still lost in our sins, the dead in Christ have perished, and we are the most pitiful people on earth (verse 19).

What is the biblical evidence that Jesus rose from the dead?

Jesus first attested to His resurrection by appearing to Mary Magdalene (John 20:1,10-14)—a fact that is a highly significant indicator of the authenticity and reliability of the resurrection account. The disciples would never have invented the resurrection story this way. In first-century Jewish law, a woman's testimony was unacceptable except in a very few circumstances. A fabricator would have been much more likely to portray Peter or one of the other male disciples at the tomb. Why does the biblical text tell us that the Lord appeared first to Mary? Because that was the way it actually happened.

Note also that the disciples came away from the crucifixion frightened and full of doubt. Yet Jesus' resurrection appearance to the disciples transformed their lives (John 20:19-20). The cowards became bulwarks of courage, fearless defenders of the faith. Only the resurrection can account for this incredible transformation.

As the days passed, Jesus continued to make many appearances and proved He indeed had risen from the dead. Acts 1:3 says, "He showed himself to these men and gave many convincing proofs that he was alive. He appeared to them over a period of forty days and spoke about the kingdom of God." Moreover, "He appeared to more than five hundred of the brothers at the same time, most of whom are still living" (1 Corinthians 15:6). The resurrection of Christ is one of the best-attested historical events of ancient times.

How do we know the disciples didn't just make up the story about Jesus' resurrection?

It is difficult to believe that Jesus' followers—predominantly Jewish and therefore aware of God's stern commandments against lying and bearing false witness—would make up such a lie. It is even more difficult to believe they would suffer and give up their own lives to defend it.

Moreover, Paul said the resurrected Christ appeared to more than 500 people at a single time and that most of them were still alive (1 Corinthians 15:6). If Paul had misrepresented the facts, any of these 500 could have come forward to dispute his claims. But no one did because the resurrection really occurred.

Was Jesus raised from the dead physically or spiritually?

Multiple lines of evidence show that Christ was resurrected physically.

- The resurrected Christ Himself said, "See My hands and My feet, that it is I Myself; touch Me and see, for a spirit does not have flesh and bones as you see that I have" (Luke 24:39 NASB).

- In John 2:19 Christ affirmed, "Destroy this temple, and I will raise it again in three days." (Jesus was referring to His body.)

- The resurrected Christ ate physical food on four different occasions to prove that He had a real physical body (Luke 24:30-31,42-43; John 21:12-13; Acts 1:4).

- People touched the resurrected Christ's physical body (Matthew 28:9; Luke 24:39; John 20:17).

- The body that is "sown" in death is the very same body that is raised in life (1 Corinthians 15:35-44).

If Jesus' resurrection body was physical, how could He materialize in closed rooms (John 20:19)?

Jesus' resurrection body was material (see Luke 24:39). The fact that He could get into a room with a closed door does not demand He had to dematerialize in order to do it.

If Jesus had chosen to do so, He could have performed this same miracle before His death in His preresurrection material body. Prior to His resurrection, Jesus performed miracles with His physical body that transcended natural laws, such as walking on water (John 6:16-20). But this miracle did not prove that His preresurrection body was immaterial or that it could dematerialize. Otherwise, Peter's preresurrection walk on water would mean his body dematerialized for a moment and then quickly rematerialized (Matthew 14:29)!

Scripture indicates that the resurrection body, although physical, is supernatural (1 Corinthians 15:44). We should therefore expect that it could do supernatural things, such as appearing in a room with closed doors.

Did Jesus actually die? Might He have just passed out?

The swoon theory, which suggests that Jesus did not really die on the cross but merely fainted from exhaustion, is beyond credulity.

- Jesus endured six trials and was beaten beyond description.
- He was so weak that He could not carry the wooden crossbar.
- Huge spikes pierced His wrists and feet.
- A Roman soldier speared Him.
- Four Roman executioners confirmed that Jesus was dead.
- More than a hundred pounds of gummy spices were applied to Jesus' body, and no one saw Jesus breathing.
- A large stone weighing several tons was rolled against the tomb, a seal was wrapped across the entrance, and Roman guards were placed there.

Are we to believe that Jesus survived His torture, appeared dead to the people who crucified Him and to those who handled His body, awoke in the cool tomb, and was strong enough to split off the garments, push the several-ton stone away, and fight off the Roman guards?

Could the women and disciples have gone to the wrong tomb?

For this to happen, a lot of people would have had to go to the wrong tomb: the women, Peter and John, the Jewish leaders, the Roman soldiers, and even Joseph of Arimathea—the owner of the tomb! (The angel would also have had to be confused.)

How could Jesus have been in the tomb "three days and three nights" if He was crucified on Friday and rose on Sunday?

The Gospel accounts are clear that Jesus was crucified and buried on Friday. This means Jesus was in the grave for part of Friday, the entire Sabbath (Saturday), and part of Sunday. In other words, He was in the tomb for two full nights, one full day, and part of two days.

Jews reckoned any part of a day as an entire day. The ancient Babylonian Talmud (a set of Jewish commentaries) tells us that "the portion of a day is as the whole of it." So in Jewish reckoning, Jesus was in the tomb for three days and three nights.

Part 5

Humankind and Sin

15

The Origins of Humankind

Did humankind evolve from apes?

There are many problems with the evolutionary hypothesis. Here are six.

1. Nearly all scientists affirm that the universe had a beginning. They may disagree as to how that beginning happened, but they largely agree that it did. Intelligent design proponents affirm that a beginning implies the existence of a Beginner—a Creator. As Scripture says, "Every house is built by someone, but God is the builder of everything" (Hebrews 3:4).

2. The universe appears to have been designed. Everything is perfect for life on earth—so perfect and so finely tuned that it gives every evidence of coming from the hands of an intelligent Designer. The earth's size, composition, distance from the sun, rotational period, and many other factors are all just right for life. The chances of even

one planet having all of these factors converge by accident are almost nonexistent.

The genetic code of all biological life on earth also gives evidence of intelligent design. The information contained in genetic code is far more complex than the information stored in computer software programs. The complex design implies the existence of a Designer.

3. The fossil records do not support evolution—in fact, they provide evidence against it. If evolution were true, progressively complex evolutionary forms in the fossil records would reveal transitions that took place. But no such evidence exists. No transitional links have been discovered in the fossil records.

4. The theory of evolution assumes a long series of positive upward mutations. In almost all known cases, however, mutations are not beneficial but are harmful to living beings and often lead to death. Deformities typically lessen the survival potential of an animal instead of strengthening it. Even if a few good mutations took place, the incredible number of damaging mutations would utterly overwhelm the good ones.

5. The first and second laws of thermodynamics are foundational to science and have never been contradicted in nature. The first law says that matter and energy are not created or destroyed; they just change forms. The second law says that in an isolated system (such as our universe), the natural course of things is to degenerate. The universe is running down, not evolving upward.

6. Evolutionists often make false claims. Some have claimed that scientific evidence supports the theory of evolution. These individuals generally appeal to the fact that mutations within species (*microevolution*) are a proven scientific fact. But to say that mutations within species constitute evidence for mutations or transformations into entirely new species (*macroevolution*) requires an incredible leap of logic.

Is theistic evolution a biblical concept?

The theory of theistic evolution has a number of serious problems. For one thing, it makes a complete allegory out of Genesis 1:1–2:4, for which there is no warrant. Certainly the suggestion that humanity is derived from a nonhuman ancestor cannot be reconciled with the explicit statement of man's creation in Genesis 2:7. Further, if Adam was not a real historical person, the analogy between Christ and Adam in Romans 5:12-21 utterly breaks down.

Certainly Christ believed in a literal creation of Adam and Eve (Matthew 19:4; Mark 10:6). (Christ would know, for He is the actual Creator—John 1:3; Colossians 1:16; Hebrews 1:2,10.) If His words cannot be trusted in these particulars, how can anyone trust His words in other matters?

Are the soul and the spirit the same?

This is a much-debated issue. The dichotomist view is

that man is composed of two parts—material (body) and immaterial (soul/spirit). In this view, soul and spirit are essentially the same. Man's entire immaterial part is called *soul* in 1 Peter 2:11, and it's called *spirit* in James 2:26. The terms appear to be interchangeable.

In the trichotomist view, the soul and spirit are separate entities, and man consists of three realities—body, soul, and spirit. Trichotomists generally say that the body involves world-consciousness, the soul involves self-consciousness, and the spirit involves God-consciousness. They are listed separately in 1 Thessalonians 5:23 and Hebrews 4:12.

Perhaps a few distinctions would be helpful. If we are talking about mere substance, we must conclude that man has only a material and an immaterial aspect. However, if we are talking about function, we may say that man's immaterial aspect has a number of functions, including those of soul and spirit. Other components of man's immaterial nature include the heart (Hebrews 4:12; Matthew 22:37), the conscience (Hebrews 10:22; 1 Peter 2:19), and the mind (Romans 12:2).

What does the Bible say about the equality of the races?

God created all races of man. All human beings are completely equal in terms of their creation (Genesis 1:27), the sin problem (Romans 3:23), God's love for them (John 3:16), and God's provision of salvation for them (Matthew 28:19). The apostle Paul affirmed, "From one man he made every nation of men, that they should inhabit the whole earth; and he determined the times set for them and the exact places where they should live" (Acts 17:26).

What does the Bible say about the equality of the sexes?

Jesus had a very high view of women. In a Jewish culture where women were discouraged from studying the law, Jesus taught women and men as equals (Matthew 14:21; 15:38). And He often featured women and their activities when illustrating the character of the kingdom of God (Luke 13:20-21; 15:8-10; 17:35).

Galatians 3:28 tells us that there is neither male nor female in Jesus Christ. First Peter 3:7 says men and women are fellow heirs of grace. Verses such as these show that men and women are spiritually equal. Nevertheless, Scripture also speaks of male leadership in the family and in the church (Ephesians 5:22; 1 Corinthians 11:3; 14:34; 1 Timothy 2:11).

16

Man Related to God

How can we reconcile man's free will and God's sovereignty?

Scripture portrays God as absolutely sovereign (Psalm

135:6; Ephesians 1:11). Scripture also portrays man as having a free will (Genesis 3:1-7). Our understanding is finite, so we are not able to comprehend how both divine sovereignty and human free will can be true, but Scripture teaches both doctrines. In fact, they are often side by side in single Scripture verses.

For example, in Acts 2:23 we read of Jesus, "This man was handed over to you by God's set purpose and foreknowledge; and you, with the help of wicked men, put him to death by nailing him to the cross." Here we see both divine sovereignty and human free will.

We see both doctrines in Acts 13:48 as well: "When the Gentiles heard this, they were glad and honored the word of the Lord; and all who were appointed for eternal life believed." God's sovereignty is clear as is man's free will.

Divine sovereignty and human free will may be like parallel railroad tracks that run side by side in Scripture without coming together this side of eternity. When we enter glory, we will no doubt come to a fuller understanding of these biblical doctrines. Now we see but a poor reflection as in a mirror; then we shall see clearly (1 Corinthians 13:12).

If God is sovereign, why should we pray?

God is sovereign over all things (Ephesians 1:4-5,11). He has ordained not only the ends but also the means to those ends. In other words, God has not only sovereignly ordained to bring certain things about but also ordained to accomplish certain things as a result of the prayers of His people. So we should most definitely pray for specific needs (see Philippians 4:6) and never forget the scriptural teaching that we do not have because we do not ask God (James 4:2).

How can God say He loves Jacob but hates Esau (Romans 9:13)?

The word *hate* should not be taken to mean that God had the human emotional sense of disgust or disdain, or that He had a desire for revenge against Esau. God did not have a negative psychological emotion that burned against Esau. Rather, the word should be understood as a Hebrew idiom that means "to love less" (Genesis 29:30-33).

Did God harden Pharaoh's heart but hold him accountable (Exodus 4:21-23)?

Ten times, Scripture says that Pharaoh hardened his own heart (Exodus 7:13-14,22; 8:15,19,32; 9:7,34-35; 13:15), and ten times, Scripture says that God hardened Pharaoh's heart (4:21; 7:3; 9:12; 10:1,20,27; 11:10; 14:4,8,17). In Romans 9:17-18 the apostle Paul uses this as an example of the inscrutable will of God and of His mercy toward human beings. Pharaoh hardened his own heart seven times before God first hardened it, though the prediction that God would do it preceded all.

God hardens on the same grounds that He shows mercy. If men will accept mercy, He will give it to them. If they will not, thus hardening themselves, He is only just and righteous in judging them. Mercy is the effect of a right attitude, and hardening is the effect of stubbornness or a wrong attitude toward God. The same sunshine hardens the clay and softens the wax. The responsibility is with the materials, not with the sun. Scholars have suggested that the danger of resisting God is that He will eventually give us over to our own choices (see Romans 1:24-28).

Does God change His mind (1 Samuel 15:11) or not (verse 29)?

On the one hand, God's essence or nature is unchanging (Malachi 3:6). So are His eternal purposes (see Ephesians 1). But this does not mean that God cannot interact with His creatures and respond to them.

God promised to judge the Ninevites but then withheld judgment after the entire city repented (Jonah 3). Many people fail to realize that God has what you might call a built-in cancelation clause to His promises of blessing or judgment. This clause is found in Jeremiah 18:7-10. If people repent, He withholds judgment. If they do evil, He reconsiders the good He had intended to do.

This indicates that God changes some of His actions when people change their actions. He is a God of mercy. When He sees repentance, He responds with mercy and grace.

Does God always heal when Christians pray for healing?

No. Sometimes God may have something He wants

to teach believers by allowing them to go through times of sickness. God allowed Epaphroditus (Philippians 2:25-27), Trophimus (2 Timothy 4:20), Timothy (1 Timothy 5:23), Job (Job 1–2), and Paul (2 Corinthians 12:7-9) to suffer periods of sickness.

The healing of our bodies in our mortal state is not guaranteed in the atonement, but ultimate healing (in our resurrection bodies) *is* guaranteed in the atonement. Our resurrection bodies will never get sick, grow old, or die (see 1 Corinthians 15:50-55).

17

The Sin Problem

What is original sin?

Adam and Eve's sin affect the entire human race. The apostle Paul said that "sin entered the world through one man, and death through sin, and in this way death came to all men, because all sinned...Through the disobedience of the one man the many were made sinners" (Romans 5:12,19; see also 1 Corinthians 15:21-22).

Was death the result of sin?

Yes. Scripture reveals a direct connection between sin and death (Romans 5:12). One causes the other. Death came into the universe as a result of sin (Genesis 2:17).

This means that death is not natural. It is an unnatural intruder. God intended human beings to live. Death is therefore foreign and hostile to human life. Death has arisen because of our rebellion against God; it is a form of God's judgment.

But there is grace even in death. As a judgment against sin, death prevents us from living forever in a state of sin. God saw to it that man's existence in a state of sin had definite limits. And by sending a Savior into the world—the Lord Jesus Christ—God made provision for taking care of the sin problem altogether (John 4:42). Those who believe in Him will live eternally at His side, the sin problem having been banished forever.

Does God punish children for their parents' sins?

The primary verse of dispute is Numbers 14:18, where we read that the Lord "punishes the children for the sin of the fathers to the third and fourth generation." In Deuteronomy 24:16, however, we read, "Fathers shall not be put to death for their children, nor children put to death for their fathers; each is to die for his own sin." Moreover, in Ezekiel 18:14-20 we read that children will not die for the sins of their fathers.

Numbers 14:18 is probably referring to the fact that parents pass on to their children sinful patterns of behavior. We are told that Ahaziah "did evil in the eyes of the LORD, because he walked in the ways of his father and mother" (1 Kings 22:52). His mother "encouraged him in doing wrong" (2 Chronicles 22:3). Similarly, in Jeremiah

9:14 we read of those who "followed the Baals, as their fathers taught them."

What is the "sin that leads to death" (1 John 5:16)?

Some believe the "sin that leads to death" refers to the spiritual death of unbelievers. Others say it refers to the physical death of believers as a result of either committing one particular sin or persistently committing any sin without repenting.

From my understanding of John's writings, the sin that leads to death might be viewed as a permanent separation of the believer into the *kosmos* (the fallen anti-God world system), which subsequently ends up killing him. There is a close relationship in John's writings between sin, death, and the *kosmos*. The *kosmos* is characterized by sin and is, in fact, a death-system. To become a part of this system and remain entrenched there is subsequently to come within the grips of death.

Seen in this way, the sin for which death is a consequence is permanently retrogressing into the *kosmos* death-system. Other individual sins—whether related to lust of the flesh, lust of the eyes, or the pride of life—can be committed that will not likely end in death. But in light of the fact that these lesser sins are a part of the *kosmos* system, it is possible that if people don't repent but persist in a sin, it could ultimately lead them to commit the greater sin of total separation into the *kosmos* death-system. In such a condition, the *kosmos* ends up killing the believer. The death-system yields its fruit—death.

Part 6

Salvation

18

The Gospel of Salvation

Are the heathen really lost?

Yes. If the heathen are not really lost, many of Christ's teachings become absurd. John 3:16, for example, says, "For God so loved the world that he gave his one and only Son, that whoever believes in him shall not perish but have eternal life." This verse becomes meaningless if the heathen are not lost.

If the heathen are not lost, Christ's postresurrection and preascension commands to His disciples are a mockery. In Luke 24:27 (NKJV) Christ commanded that "repentance and remission of sins should be preached in His name to all nations." Similarly, in Matthew 28:19, Christ gave the Great Commission. These verses might well be stricken from Scripture if human beings without Christ are not lost.

If the heathen do not need Christ and His salvation,

neither do we. Conversely, if we need Him, so do they. The Scriptures become a bundle of contradictions, the Savior becomes a false teacher, and the Christian message becomes much ado about nothing if the heathen are not lost.

Scripture makes it very plain: "Salvation is found in no one else, for there is no other name under heaven given to men by which we must be saved" (Acts 4:12). "There is one God and one mediator between God and men, the man Christ Jesus" (1 Timothy 2:5).

Does the Bible teach that all humanity will eventually be saved?

Certain passages—John 12:32; Philippians 2:10-11; and 1 Timothy 2:4—are typically twisted out of context in support of universalism. Such passages, interpreted properly, do not support universalism.

John 12:32 says that Christ's work on the cross makes possible the salvation of both Jews and Gentiles. Notice, however, that the Lord—in the same passage—warned of judgment of those who reject Christ (verse 48).

Philippians 2:10-11 assures us that someday all people will acknowledge Jesus as Lord but not necessarily as Savior. (Even those in hell will have to acknowledge Christ's lordship.)

First Timothy 2:4 expresses God's desire that all be saved, but it does not promise that all will be. This divine desire is realized only in those who exercise faith in Christ (Acts 16:31).

The Scriptures consistently categorize people into one of two classes—believers and unbelievers—and portray the final destiny of every person in one of two realities—heaven or hell. In Matthew 13:49 Jesus said, "This is how it will be at the end of the age. The angels will come and separate the wicked from the righteous." Two classes are mentioned (unbelievers and believers), and they have different destinies (hell for unbelievers, heaven for believers). (See also Matthew 25:32-46.)

What is the gospel?

The best definition of the gospel is found in 1 Corinthians 15:3-4: "For what I received I passed on to you as of first importance: that Christ died for our sins according to the Scriptures, that he was buried, that he was raised on the third day according to the Scriptures."

The Gospel, according to this passage, has four components: (1) man is a sinner, (2) Christ is the Savior, (3) Christ died as man's substitute, and (4) Christ rose from the dead. This is the gospel Paul and the other apostles preached and the gospel we too must preach.

What are some faulty concepts of the gospel?

People have had a number of misconceptions about the gospel. Some have taught that one must plead for mercy to be saved. However, this idea is never found in Scripture. Salvation comes by faith in Christ (John 3:16; Acts 16:31). God provides pardon for anyone who believes; no one has to plead for it.

Others have taught that we must follow Christ's example and seek to live as He lived in order to be a Christian. *The Imitation of Christ* by Thomas à Kempis has been understood by many to teach that we become Christians by living as Christ did and obeying His teachings, seeking to behave as He behaved. From a scriptural perspective, we simply do not have it in us to live as Christ lived. We are fallen human beings (Romans 3:23). Only the Holy Spirit working in us can imitate Christ in our lives (Galatians 5:16-23).

Still others have inadvertently communicated that prayer is a necessary component in becoming saved. In other words, one must pray the "prayer of repentance." The scriptural perspective is that even though prayer may be a vehicle for the expression of one's faith, it is the faith that brings about salvation, not the prayer through which that faith is communicated. In fact, one can bypass prayer altogether by simply exercising faith in one's heart and be saved at that moment.

We must always remember that salvation is a gift that we receive by faith in Christ (Ephesians 2:8-9). This is the glorious message of the gospel.

What is justification?

Humankind's dilemma of falling short pointed to the need for a solution—and that solution is justification (Romans 3:24). The word *justified* is a legal term that means "declared righteous" or "acquitted." Negatively, the word means that man is once-for-all pronounced not guilty before God. Positively, it means that man is once-for-all pronounced righteous. Christ's own righteousness is imputed to the believer's life. From the moment we place our faith in Christ, God sees us through the lens of Christ's righteousness (Romans 3:28; 5:1; 10:10; Galatians 2:16).

After death, do unbelievers have a second chance to be saved?

No. But two verses are often misinterpreted in regard to this issue—1 Peter 3:18-19 and 1 Peter 4:6. Let us take a brief look at each.

1 Peter 3:18-19. This passage says, "For Christ...was put to death in the body but made alive by the Spirit, through whom also he went and preached to the spirits in prison." Difficult passages like this must be interpreted according to the clearer passages of Scripture. The clear passages of Scripture tell us that immediately following the moment of death comes the judgment (Hebrews 9:27). There is no possibility of redemption beyond death's door (Luke 16:19-31).

Many scholars believe the "spirits in prison" in 1 Peter 3:19 are fallen angels who grievously sinned against God. The Greek word in this verse translated *preach* (*kerusso*) is not the word used for preaching the gospel but rather points to a proclamation—as in a proclamation of victory. This passage may imply that the powers of darkness thought they had destroyed Jesus at the crucifixion, but God raised Him from the dead and turned the tables on them—and Jesus Himself proclaimed their doom.

Another possible interpretation is that between His death and resurrection, Jesus went to the place of the dead and preached to the wicked contemporaries of Noah (see verse 20). The preaching, however, was not a gospel message but rather a proclamation of victory.

Still others believe this passage teaches that Christ preached through the historical person of Noah to those who, because they rejected Noah's message, are now spirits in prison. First Peter 1:11 says the Spirit of Christ spoke through the Old Testament prophets. And Noah is later described as a "preacher of righteousness" (2 Peter 2:5). So the Spirit of Christ may have preached through Noah to the ungodly humans who, at the time of Peter's writing, were now spirits in prison awaiting final judgment.

Regardless of which position is correct, the passage does not teach that people can hear and respond to the Gospel of salvation in the next life.

1 Peter 4:6. This verse says, "For this is the reason the gospel was preached even to those who are now dead, so that they might be judged according to men in regard to the body, but live according to God in regard to the spirit."

This verse refers to those who are now dead but who heard the Gospel while they were yet alive. This especially makes sense in view of the tenses used: The Gospel was preached (in the past) to those who are dead (presently).

Is Jesus one of many ways to God?

Jesus said He is humanity's only means of coming into

a relationship with God (John 14:6). Peter and Paul made this equally clear (Acts 4:12; 1 Timothy 2:5). Jesus sternly warned His followers about those who would try to set forth a different Christ (Matthew 24:4-5).

19

Eternal Security

Is it true that people are saved because of their faith in Christ and not because of the things they do?

Close to 200 times, the New Testament states that salvation is by faith alone—with no other behaviors in sight. Consider these examples:

- "Everyone who believes in him may have eternal life" (John 3:15).

- "I tell you the truth, whoever hears my word and believes him who sent me has eternal life and will not be condemned; he has crossed over from death to life" (John 5:24).

- "I am the resurrection and the life. He who believes in me will live, even though he dies" (John 11:25).

- "I have come into the world as a light, so that no one who believes in me should stay in darkness" (John 12:46).

- "These [miraculous signs] are written that you
  may believe that Jesus is the Christ, the Son
  of God, and that by believing you may have
  life in his name" (John 20:31).

If salvation were not by faith alone, Jesus' message in
the Gospel of John would be deceptive because Jesus gives
only one condition for salvation (faith), not two (faith
and works).

What do James 2:17,26 mean when they say that faith without action, or deeds, is dead?

Martin Luther said it best: James 2 is not teaching that
a person is saved by works. A person is justified (declared
righteous before God) by faith alone, but not by a faith
that is alone. In other words, genuine faith will always
result in good works in the saved person's life.

James is writing to Jewish Christians ("the twelve
tribes"—James 1:1) who were in danger of giving nothing but lip service to Jesus. His intent, therefore, is to dis-
tinguish true faith from false faith. He shows that true
faith results in works, which become visible evidences of
faith's invisible presence. In other words, good works are
the "vital signs" indicating that faith is alive.

What is the "lordship salvation" issue all about?

The lordship salvation debate focuses on these questions: What is the nature of salvation and saving faith?
What does it mean to receive Jesus as Lord and Savior?

Lordship salvation advocates say that in order to be saved, people must not only acknowledge that Christ is Savior but also be willing to submit to His lordship. In other words, at the moment they trust in Christ for salvation, they must choose to commit their lives absolutely to the Lord even though the actual practice of a committed life may not follow immediately or completely.

Non-lordship proponents argue that such a presalvation commitment to Christ's lordship compromises salvation by grace ("unmerited favor"). They argue that "accepting Jesus as Lord" refers not to a subjective commitment to Christ's lordship but rather to repentance (a changing of one's mind) about one's ideas of who Christ is (Messiah-God) and exercising personal faith in Him. Repentance from sin follows in the Christian's daily walk with the Lord.

Martin Luther gives us a good insight on this issue. He said that faith alone justifies, but not the faith that is alone. He said that true faith will not fail to produce good works, just as the sun will not cease to give light.

What does the Bible say about our eternal security in salvation?

When people exercise saving faith in Jesus Christ, they are forever in the family of God. God never kicks anyone out of His eternal family.

First Corinthians 12:13 explains that at the moment of salvation, the Holy Spirit places us in the body of Christ.

Once we are infused into the body of Christ, we are never excised from it.

Ephesians 1:13 and 4:30 indicate that at the moment of believing in Jesus Christ for salvation, we are permanently sealed by the Holy Spirit. At that point, we are God's everlasting property. That seal guarantees that we will make it to heaven.

John 10:28-30 highlights the Father's purpose—to keep us secure despite anything that might happen once we have trusted in Christ. Nothing can snatch us out of His hands. God's plans cannot be thwarted (Isaiah 14:24).

Romans 8:29-39 portrays an unbroken chain that spans from the predestination of believers to their glorification in heaven. This indicates the certainty of all believers reaching heaven.

We should remember that Christ regularly prays for each Christian (Hebrews 7:25). With Jesus interceding for us, we are secure. (His prayers are always answered!)

Of course, the fact that believers are secure in their salvation does not mean they are free to sin. If Christians don't turn from their sin, Scripture says that God will discipline them just as a father disciplines his children (see Hebrews 12:7-11).

Does Hebrews 6:4-6 teach that Christians can lose their salvation?

Christians disagree over this passage, but I personally do not think it indicates a Christian can lose salvation. The verse is not dealing with falling away from salvation but falling away from maturity in Christ. That is why verse 1 exhorts believers to "go on to maturity."

This was an important issue for the Jews of the first century who had converted to Christ and become Christians. These Jewish believers in Christ were being heavily persecuted by other Jews, and this caused them to become a bit gun-shy in their Christian lives. Perhaps they thought that if they kept quiet about their faith and withdrew from external involvement in Christian affairs, the Jewish high priest might lighten up on them.

The author of the book of Hebrews saw this as a retreat from spiritual maturity in Christ. He thus encouraged them to move on to maturity in Christ.

So Hebrews 6:4-6 is not saying, "Shape up, or you'll lose your salvation." Rather, it is saying, "You're already in the school of Christ and have made a commitment, so let's move on to maturity." This was an important message for those first-century Jewish converts to hear.

20

God's Part, Man's Part

Is God's election of people to salvation based on His foreknowledge or on His divine sovereignty?

This is a complicated and much-debated issue. Let us take a brief look at both views.

The first view is that God's election is based on His foreknowledge. This view says that God used His foreknowledge to look down the corridors of time to see who would respond favorably to His gospel message, and on that basis He elected certain persons to salvation. The argument for this view goes like this:

- Scripture teaches that God's salvation has appeared to all men, not merely the elect (Titus 2:11).

- The Bible teaches that Christ died for all (1 Timothy 2:6; 4:10; Hebrews 2:9; 2 Peter 2:1; 1 John 2:2).

- Scripture often exhorts everyone to turn to God (Isaiah 31:6; Joel 2:13-14; Matthew 18:3; Acts 3:19), to repent (Matthew 3:2; Luke 13:3,5; Acts 2:38; 17:30), and to believe (John 6:29; Acts 16:31; 1 John 3:23).

- Scripture seems to indicate that election is based on God's foreknowledge of who would respond positively to such exhortations (Romans 8:28-30; 1 Peter 1:1-2).

However, some substantial arguments challenge this view. To begin, the Father evidently gave certain ones to Christ (John 6:37; 17:2,6,9). Christ said, "No one can come to me unless the Father who sent me draws him"

(John 6:44). Moreover, in Romans 9:10-16, Paul reminds us that God chose Jacob rather than Esau before they were born.

We read in Acts 13:48 that "all who were appointed to eternal life believed." Ephesians 1:5-8 and 2:8-10 represent salvation as originating in God's choice and as being all of grace (see also Acts 5:31; 11:18; Romans 12:3; 2 Timothy 2:25). Finally, many claim that if election is not unconditional and absolute, God's whole plan is uncertain and liable to miscarriage.

The second view (my view) is that God's election is based on His sovereign choice and not on His foreknowledge of people's choices. Here are some arguments for this view:

- Many biblical statements highlight God's choice to elect people (Acts 13:48).

- The entire process of salvation is a gift of God (Romans 12:3; Ephesians 2:8-10).

- The Father gives people to Christ (John 6:37; 17:2) and draws them to Him (John 6:44).

- God clearly sovereignly called some individuals, such as Paul (Galatians 1:15) and Jeremiah (Jeremiah 1:5), even before they were born.

- Election is necessary in light of man's total depravity (Romans 3:10-20) and inability (Ephesians 2:1).

- Election is compatible with God's sovereignty
  (Proverbs 19:21; Jeremiah 10:23).

- God gave us His grace before the beginning
  of time (2 Timothy 1:9).

- Election by choice is the basis and motivation
  for godly living (Colossians 3:12; 2 Thessalonians 2:13; 1 Peter 2:9).

Two primary arguments have been suggested against
this view. First, a limited election seems to require a limited atonement, which Scripture clearly refutes (John 1:29;
3:16; 1 Timothy 2:6; Hebrews 2:9; and 1 John 2:2).

Second, election by choice seems to make God responsible for reprobation. However, those not included
in election suffer only their due reward. God does not
elect people to hell. Those not elected to salvation are left
to their own self-destructive ways.

Regardless of whether God's election is based on His
foreknowledge of our choices or on His own choice, we
should remember these facts:

- God's election is loving (Ephesians 1:4-11).

- Election glorifies God (Ephesians 1:12-14).

- The product of election is a people who do
  good works (Ephesians 2:10; see also Colossians 3:12; Romans 11:33-36).

What is limited atonement?

Limited atonement (a doctrine I disagree with) is the view that Christ's atoning death was only for the elect and not for all people. Here are some of the key verses advocates of limited atonement cite in favor of their position.

- Matthew 1:21: "She will give birth to a son, and you are to give him the name Jesus, because he will save *his people* from their sins."

- Matthew 20:28: "The Son of Man did not come to be served, but to serve, and to give his life as a ransom *for many*."

- Matthew 26:28: "This is my blood of the covenant, which is poured out *for many* for the forgiveness of sins."

- John 10:15: "I lay down my life *for the sheep*."

- Acts 20:28: "Keep watch over yourselves and all the flock of which the Holy Spirit has made you overseers. Be shepherds of *the church* of God, which he bought with his own blood."

- Ephesians 5:25: "Husbands, love your wives, just as Christ loved *the church* and gave himself up for *her*."

- Hebrews 9:28: "So Christ was sacrificed once to take away the sins of *many people*; and he

will appear a second time, not to bear sin, but
to bring salvation to those who are waiting
for him."

- John 15:13: "Greater love has no one than this,
that he lay down his life *for his friends*."

Here are eight arguments offered by proponents of
this viewpoint:

1. The Bible says Christ died for a specific group of
people—His sheep (John 10:11,15), His church
(Acts 20:28; Ephesians 5:25-27), His people
(Matthew 1:21).

2. The elect were chosen before the foundation
of the world (Ephesians 1), so Christ could not
have died for all human beings.

3. Some advocates of limited atonement say
Christ is defeated if He died for all men and all
men are not saved.

4. Some advocates of limited atonement say that if
Christ died for all people, God would be unfair
in sending people to hell for their own sins.

5. Christ did not pray for everyone in His high
priestly prayer in John 17, but prayed only for
His own, so He must not have died for everyone.

6. Some advocates of limited atonement have

charged that unlimited atonement tends toward universalism.

7. In the Middle Ages, such scholars as Prosper of Aquitaine, Thomas Bradwardine, and John Staupitz taught limited atonement. John Calvin did not explicitly teach the doctrine, but it may be implicit in some of his writings.

8. Though Scripture uses such terms as *all*, *world*, and *whosoever* in reference to those for whom Christ died (for example, John 3:16), these words are to be understood in terms of the elect. In other words, *all* refers to all of the elect or all classes of men (Jew and Gentile). Similarly, the word *world* refers to the world of the elect or to people without distinction (Jews and Gentiles).

Is unlimited atonement scriptural?

I believe that the doctrine of unlimited atonement— that is, the view that Christ died for all people—is the scriptural view and that numerous verses support it.

"The Son of Man came to seek and to save what was lost" (Luke 19:10). The lost in this verse refers to the collective whole of lost humanity, not just to the lost elect.

Jesus is "the Lamb of God, who takes away the sin of the world" (John 1:29). "The world" seems to refer indiscriminately to the whole human race.

"For God so loved the world that he gave his one and

only Son, that whoever believes in him shall not perish but have eternal life" (John 3:16). In the two previous verses, Christ alludes to Numbers 21, where Moses sets up the brazen serpent in the camp of Israel so that anyone could look to it and be healed. In verse 15 Christ applies the story spiritually when He says that everyone who believes in the Son of Man will experience spiritual deliverance.

In John 4:42 some Samaritan people said to the Samaritan woman, "We no longer believe just because of what you said; now we have heard for ourselves, and we know that this man really is the Savior of the world." Obviously, the Samaritans were not referring to the world of the elect.

First Timothy 4:10 speaks of Jesus as "the Savior of all men, and especially of those who believe." There is a clear distinction in this verse between all men and those who believe. Christ has made a provision of salvation for all men, though it becomes effective only for those who exercise faith in Christ.

Romans 5:6 says that "Christ died for the ungodly." To read this as saying that Christ died for the ungodly among the elect doesn't make much sense. Rather, the verse plainly indicates that Christ died for all the ungodly of the earth.

First John 2:2 says, "He is the atoning sacrifice for our sins, and not only for ours but also for the sins of the whole world."

Isaiah 53:6 says, "We all, like sheep, have gone astray, each of us has turned to his own way; and the LORD has laid on him the iniquity of us all." The Lord died for all those who went astray.

In 2 Peter 2:1, we learn that Christ even paid the price of redemption for false teachers who deny Him. This verse seems to point out quite clearly that there is a distinction between those for whom Christ died and those who are finally saved.

Many verses indicate that we are to proclaim the gospel to all human beings (Matthew 24:14; 28:19; Acts 1:8). If Christ died only for the elect, how could God offer salvation to all persons without some sort of insincerity, artificiality, or dishonesty?

How do we put the "limited" and "unlimited" verses together so that, taken as a whole, all the verses are interpreted in a harmonious way without contradicting each other? The two sets of passages—one seemingly in support of limited atonement, the other in support of unlimited atonement—are not irreconcilable. The benefits of Christ's death belong only to God's sheep, His people, and the like, but Christ would have to have died only for them in order for limited atonement to be true. No one denies that Christ died for God's sheep and His people, only that Christ died *exclusively* for them. Certainly if Christ died for the whole of humanity, we can say He died for a specific part of the whole.

21

The Role of Baptism

**Which is the correct mode of baptism,
immersion or sprinkling?**

Christians are divided on this issue. Those who argue
for sprinkling point out that a secondary meaning of the
Greek word *baptizo* is "to bring under the influence of."
This fits sprinkling better than immersion. Moreover, they
say baptism by sprinkling better pictures the coming of
the Holy Spirit upon a person.

Some people also suggest that immersion would have
been impossible in some of the baptisms portrayed in
Scripture. In Acts 2:41, for example, it would have been
impossible to immerse all 3000 people who were baptized. The same is said to be true in regard to Acts 8:38,
10:47, and 16:33.

Those who hold to the immersion view (as I do)
respond by pointing out that the primary meaning of the
Greek word *baptizo* is "to immerse." And the prepositions
normally used in conjunction with *baptizo* (such as *into*
and *out of* the water) clearly picture immersion and not
sprinkling. The Greek language has perfectly acceptable
words for sprinkling and pouring, but these words are
never used in the context of baptism in the New Testament.

The ancient Jews practiced baptism by immersion. The

Jewish converts to Christianity (including the apostles, who were Jews) would have been likely to follow this precedent.

Certainly baptism by immersion best pictures the significance of death to the old life and resurrection to the new life in Christ (Romans 6:1-4). And despite what advocates of sprinkling may say, in every instance of water baptism recorded in the New Testament, immersion was practiced. Arguments that not enough water was available for immersion are weak and unconvincing. Archaeologists have uncovered ancient pools throughout the Jerusalem area.

Does Acts 2:38 teach that people must be baptized in order to be saved?

The great majority of passages dealing with salvation in the New Testament affirm that salvation is by faith alone (for example, John 3:16-17). In view of such clear passages, how are we to interpret Acts 2:38?

A single word in the verse gives us the answer. "Repent and be baptized, every one of you, in the name of Jesus Christ *for* the forgiveness of your sins. And you will receive the gift of the Holy Spirit."

For is a translation of a Greek preposition (*eis*) that can indicate causality ("in order to attain") or a result ("because of"). This is an example of using *for* as a result: "I'm taking an aspirin for my headache." Obviously this means I am taking an aspirin as a result of my headache. I am not taking an aspirin in order to attain a headache.

Here's an example of using *for* as a cause: "I'm going

to the office for my paycheck." Obviously this means I am going to the office in order to get my paycheck.

Acts 2:38 uses the word *for* as a result. We might paraphrase the verse this way: "Repent and be baptized, every one of you, in the name of Jesus Christ because of (or as a result of) the remission of sins. The verse is not saying, "Repent and be baptized, every one of you, in the name of Jesus Christ in order to attain the remission of sins."

Does Mark 16:16 teach that people must be baptized in order to be saved?

I do not think so. Notice the latter part of the verse: "Whoever believes and is baptized will be saved, but whoever does not believe will be condemned." Unbelief is what brings damnation, not a lack of being baptized. People who reject the gospel, refusing to believe it, are damned.

Keep in mind the words of the apostle Paul: "For Christ did not send me to baptize, but to preach the gospel—not with words of human wisdom, lest the cross of Christ be emptied of its power" (1 Corinthians 1:17). Paul draws a clear distinction between baptism and the gospel. The Gospel is what saves (1 Corinthians 15:1-2), so baptism is clearly not necessary to attain salvation.

Does John 3:1-5 teach that people must be baptized in order to be saved?

Jesus is speaking with Nicodemus, a Pharisee who would have been trusting in his physical descent from

Abraham for entrance into the Messiah's kingdom. Christ denied such a possibility. Parents can transmit to their children only the nature they themselves possess. Because of Adam's sin, each parent's nature is sinful, so each parent transmits a sinful nature to the child. And what is sinful cannot enter the kingdom of God (verse 5). The only way one can enter God's kingdom is to experience a spiritual rebirth, and this is precisely what Jesus is emphasizing to Nicodemus.

Jesus first speaks about being born of water and the Spirit in verse 5, and then He explains what He means by this in verse 6. It would seem that *water* in verse 5 is parallel to *flesh* in verse 6, just as *Spirit* in verse 5 is parallel to *spirit* in verse 6. Jesus' message, then, is that just as one has had a physical birth to live on earth, so one must also have a spiritual birth in order to enter the kingdom of God. One must be born from above. The verse has nothing whatsoever to do with water baptism.

Is infant baptism a biblical practice?

Some people believe that infant baptism is analogous to circumcision in the Old Testament, which was done to infant boys, and that household baptisms in the New Testament must have included infants (Acts 16:33). But in the Bible, people always get baptized after their conversion experience (see Acts 16:29-34 for one of many examples). And household baptisms, such as the one described in Acts 16:33, do not specify the presence of any infants.

Of course, baptizing young children who have trusted in Christ is certainly permissible and right.

22

The Church: The Community of the Redeemed

Does being saved make one a part of the universal church?

Yes. The universal church is the ever-enlarging body of born-again believers who comprise the universal body of Christ, over which He reigns as Lord. Although the members of the church may differ in age, sex, race, wealth, social status, and ability, they are all joined together as one people (Galatians 3:28). This body is comprised only of believers in Christ. The way you become a member in this universal body is to simply place faith in Jesus Christ. If you are a believer, you are in!

Do Christians need to attend a local church?

Yes. Hebrews 10:25 specially instructs us not to forsake meeting together. The Christian life as described in Scripture is to be lived within the context of the family of God and not in isolation (Ephesians 3:14-15; Acts 2). Moreover, by attending church, we become equipped for the work of ministry (Ephesians 4:12-16). Further, when we attend church, we can receive the Lord's Supper (1 Corinthians 11:23-26). The Bible knows nothing of a "lone ranger Christian" (see Ephesians 2:19; 1 Thessalonians 5:10-11; 1 Peter 3:8).

Should we worship on Saturday or on Sunday?

We should worship on Sunday, the Lord's day. The moral principles expressed in the Ten Commandments are reaffirmed in the New Testament, but the command to set Saturday apart as a day of rest and worship is the one command that is not repeated. There are very good reasons for this.

- New Testament believers are not under the Old Testament Law (Romans 6:14; Galatians 3:24-25; 2 Corinthians 3:7,11,13; Hebrews 7:12).

- Jesus rose from the dead and appeared to some of His followers on the first day of the week—Sunday (Matthew 28:1).

- Jesus continued His appearances on succeeding Sundays (John 20:26).

- The descent of the Holy Spirit took place on a Sunday (Acts 2:1).

- The early church was thus given the pattern of Sunday worship, and this they continued to do regularly (Acts 20:7; 1 Corinthians 16:2).

- Sunday worship was further hallowed by our Lord when He appeared to John in that last great vision on the Lord's day (Revelation 1:10).

- Finally, in Colossians 2:16 we read, "There-fore do not let anyone judge you...with regard to...a Sabbath day." This verse indi-cates that the distinctive holy days of the Old Testament are no longer binding on New Testament believers.

What does the New Testament teach on tithing?

Christians today are not under the Old Testament 10 percent tithe system. In fact, we are not obligated to a per-centage tithe at all. There is not a single verse in the New Testament where God specifies that believers should give 10 percent of their income to the church.

Instead, the New Testament demonstrates a pat-tern of grace giving. We are to freely give as the Lord has freely given to us. And we are to give as we are able (2 Corinthians 8:12). For some, this will mean less than 10 percent. But for others whom God has materially blessed, this will mean much more than 10 percent.

The starting point for a right attitude toward giving to the church is to first give *ourselves* to the Lord. The early church is our example: "They gave themselves first to the Lord and then to us in keeping with God's will" (2 Corinthians 8:5). Only when we have given ourselves to the Lord will we have a proper perspective on money.

What are the different views of the Lord's Supper?

There are four primary views.

The Roman Catholic view is known as *transubstantiation*. In this view, the elements actually change into the body and blood of Jesus Christ (though their appearance doesn't change) at the prayer of the priest. The sacrament imparts grace to the recipient. Jesus Christ is literally present.

This view has a number of problems. First, Jesus was present with the disciples when He said the elements (bread and wine) were His body and blood (Luke 22:17-19). Obviously He intended that His words be taken figuratively. Besides, the Scriptures forbid the drinking of blood (Genesis 9:4; Leviticus 3:17; Acts 15:29).

The Lutheran view is known as *consubstantiation*. This view says that Christ is present *in*, *with*, and *under* the bread and wine. There is a real presence of Christ but no change in the elements. The mere partaking of the elements after the prayer of consecration communicates Christ to the participant along with the elements.

The Reformed view is that Christ is spiritually present at the Lord's Supper, and it is a means of grace. A dynamic presence of Jesus in the elements is made effective in the believer as he partakes. The partaking of His presence is not a physical eating and drinking, but an inner communion with His person.

The memorial view (my view) is that the elements do not change, and the ordinance is not intended as a means of communicating grace to the participant. The bread and wine are symbols and reminders of Jesus in His death and resurrection (1 Corinthians 11:24-25). It also reminds us of the gospel, Jesus' second coming, and our oneness as the body of Christ (verse 26; 10:17).

Part 7

Angels
and Demons

23

Angels Among Us

When did God create the angels?

God created the angels before He created the earth. Job 38:7 mentions the angels singing when the earth was created. (The NASB and other versions use the more literal translation, "sons of God," to refer to angels in Job 1:6; 2:1; 38:7.) So a vast world of spirit beings existed before the creation of the material universe. These angelic spirit beings sang as a massive choir when God created the earth.

Do all angels have wings?

Scripture indicates that many (if not all) angels have wings. The seraphim described in Isaiah 6:1-5 have wings, as do the cherubim Ezekiel saw in his vision (Ezekiel 1:6) and the angels the apostle John saw in his vision (Revelation 4:8). But other Bible verses that mention angels say nothing about wings (for example, Hebrews 13:2).

Though many angels are described as winged, we have no assurance that what is true of them is true of all angels. Since there is no explicit reference indicating that angels as a whole are winged, we must regard this as an inference at best.

How many angels are there?

Thomas Aquinas believed there are many times more angels than there are human beings. Saint Albert the Great calculated that there were exactly 399,920,004 angels. The Kabbalists of medieval Judaism determined there were precisely 301,655,722 angels.

Clement of Alexandria in the second century AD suggested that there are as many angels as there are stars in the stellar heavens (since angels are associated with the stars—Job 38:7; Psalm 148:1-3; Revelation 9:1-2; 12:3-4,7-9).

Scripture does not tell us precisely how many angels there are but does indicate that their number is vast indeed. Scripture makes reference to "a great company of the heavenly host" (Luke 2:13), and "tens of thousands and thousands of thousands" of angels (Psalm 68:17). Daniel 7:10 refers to "thousands upon thousands...ten thousand times ten thousand" (see also Revelation 5:11). That's at least 100,000,000—a number almost too vast to fathom. Job 25:3 understandably asks, "Can his forces be numbered?"

Does God need angels in order to accomplish His work in the universe?

No, God does not need angels. God uses angels not

out of necessity but rather because He sovereignly chooses to. He created them for His own pleasure and glory to carry out various functions in His ordered universe and before His throne.

Does each Christian have a single guardian angel?

Two primary passages in the New Testament relate to the idea of guardian angels. Matthew 18:10 says, "See that you do not look down on one of these little ones. For I tell you that their angels in heaven always see the face of my Father in heaven."

And in Acts 12:15, a woman named Rhoda recognized Peter's voice outside the door of the house, but the others inside—thinking Peter was still in jail—said, "You're out of your mind…It must be his angel." Some people have concluded from these two verses that every believer must have his or her own guardian angel.

This is certainly possible. However, many theologians argue that these verses are flimsy support for such an idea. (For example, the angels of the little ones in Matthew 18:10 are in heaven, not with the little ones.) Scripture seems to indicate that many multitudes of angels are always ready and willing to render help and protection to each individual Christian whenever necessary. Psalm 91:9-11 tells us, "If you make the Most High your dwelling…He will command his angels concerning you to guard you in all your ways."

24

The Devil and His Fallen Angels

How did Lucifer fall and become Satan?

Many scholars believe Ezekiel 28 and Isaiah 14 provide insights regarding how Lucifer fell and became Satan. The being described in Ezekiel 28 was a cherub on the holy mount of God (verse 14) who was initially blameless (verse 15). In fact, this cherub was "the model of perfection, full of wisdom and perfect in beauty" (verse 12). But the cherub sinned and was driven from the mountain of God (verse 16) and thrown to the earth (verse 17). Such things cannot be said of a mere human being, so many people believe this is a reference to Lucifer.

What was his iniquity? We read in verse 17, "Your heart became proud on account of your beauty, and you corrupted your wisdom because of your splendor." Lucifer apparently became so impressed with his own beauty, intelligence, power, and position that he desired for himself the honor and glory that belonged to God alone. The sin that corrupted Lucifer was self-generated pride. This seems to be confirmed in Isaiah 14:12-17, which lists Lucifer's five boastful "I will" statements.

God rightfully judged this mighty angelic being: "I threw you to the earth" (Ezekiel 28:17). As a result of Lucifer's heinous sin, he was banished from living in heaven

(Isaiah 14:12). He became corrupt, and his name changed from Lucifer (morning star) to Satan (adversary). His power became completely perverted (Isaiah 14:12,16-17). And his destiny, following the second coming of Christ, is to be bound in a pit during the thousand-year millennial kingdom over which Christ will rule (Revelation 20:3). Eventually he will be thrown into the lake of fire (Matthew 25:41).

Where did the demons come from?

Many scholars believe the first four verses of Revelation 12 contain a minihistory of Satan and the demons. Verse 4 refers to the fall of the angels who followed Satan: "[Satan's] tail swept a third of the stars out of the sky and flung them to the earth." The word *stars* is sometimes used of angels in the Bible (see Job 38:7). If *stars* refers to angels in Revelation 12:4, then after Lucifer rebelled against God, he was apparently able to draw a third of the angelic realm after him in this rebellion. He did not sin alone, but evidently led a massive angelic revolt against God.

Can Christians become demon-possessed?

A Christian cannot be possessed by a demon because he is perpetually indwelt by the Holy Spirit (1 Corinthians 6:19). My old friend Walter Martin once said that when the devil knocks on the door of the Christian's heart, the Holy Spirit opens it and says, "Get lost!"

Scripture never mentions a Christian being demon

possessed. It does include examples of Christians being afflicted by the devil but not possessed by the devil.

Christians have been delivered from Satan's domain. Christ "has rescued us from the dominion of darkness and brought us into the kingdom of the Son he loves" (Colossians 1:13). We must remember that "the one who is in you is greater than the one who is in the world" (1 John 4:4). This statement would not make much sense if Christians could be possessed by the devil.

What can Satan do to Christians?

Satan tempts believers to sin (Ephesians 2:1-3; 1 Thessalonians 3:5), to lie (Acts 5:3), and to commit sexually immoral acts (1 Corinthians 7:5). He accuses and slanders believers (Revelation 12:10), hinders their work (1 Thessalonians 2:18), sows tares among them (Matthew 13:38-39), and incites persecutions against them (Revelation 2:10).

Satan wages war against believers (Ephesians 6:11-12), opposes them with the ferociousness of a hungry lion (1 Peter 5:8), plants doubt in their minds (Genesis 3:1-5), fosters spiritual pride in their hearts (1 Timothy 3:6), and leads them away from a "sincere and pure devotion to Christ" (2 Corinthians 11:3).

Is illness always caused by demonic spirits?

On the one hand, Satan and demons can inflict people with such physical difficulties as dumbness (Matthew 9:33), blindness (12:22), and seizures (17:15-18).

They can also afflict people with mental disorders (Mark 5:4-5,15; Luke 8:27-29) and can cause people to be self-destructive (Mark 5:5; Luke 9:42).

However, Scripture distinguishes natural illnesses from demon-caused illnesses (Matthew 4:24; Mark 1:32; Luke 7:21; 9:1; Acts 5:16). In the case of numerous healings, no mention is made of demons. For example, demons aren't mentioned when Jesus healed the centurion's servant (Matthew 8:5-13). When you get sick, do not presume you are being afflicted by a demon. You may have just caught a bad bug!

What defenses does the Christian have against Satan and the powers of darkness?

God has provided spiritual armor for our defense (Ephesians 6:11-18). To wear this armor is to be characterized by such things as righteousness, obedience to the will of God, faith in God, and effective use of the Word of God.

Effective use of the Word of God is especially important for spiritual victory. Jesus used the Word of God to defeat the devil during His wilderness temptations (Matthew 4). We must learn to do the same.

Scripture specifically instructs us that each believer must be informed and thereby alert to the attacks of Satan (1 Peter 5:8). A prerequisite to defeating an enemy is to know as much as possible about the enemy—including his tactics (2 Corinthians 2:11).

We are also instructed to take a decisive stand against

Satan. James 4:7 says, "Resist the devil, and he will flee from you." This is not a one-time resistance. Rather, on a day-to-day basis we must steadfastly resist the devil. And when we do, he will flee from us. Ephesians 6:13-14 tells us to "stand firm" against the devil.

We must not give place to the devil by letting sunset pass with us having unrighteous anger in our hearts toward someone (Ephesians 4:26-27). An excess of wrath in our heart gives the devil opportunity to work in our lives.

We are instructed to rely on the indwelling Spirit of God, remembering that "the one who is in you is greater than the one who is in the world" (1 John 4:4).

We should pray for protection. Jesus set an example for us in the Lord's Prayer by teaching us to pray, "Deliver us from the evil one" (Matthew 6:13). We should also pray for each other (see Luke 22:31-32).

Of course, the believer should never dabble in the occult, for this gives the devil opportunity to work in our lives (Deuteronomy 18:10-11; Romans 16:19-20).

Finally, we must remember that Satan is "on a leash." He cannot go beyond what God will allow him (Job 1:6-12; 2:1-6). We should rest secure in the fact that God is in control of the universe and realize that Satan cannot simply do as he pleases in our lives.

Part 8

The Future

25

The Prophetic Future

When will the rapture occur?

There are four primary views. Partial rapturism is the view that only spiritual Christians will be raptured when Christ returns. Pretribulationism is the view that Christ will rapture the entire church before any part of the tribulation begins. Posttribulationism is the view that Christ will rapture the church after the tribulation. Midtribulationism is the view that Christ will rapture the church in the middle of the tribulation period.

Most Christians today are either "pretribs" or "posttribs." I am firmly convinced that the pretrib position is most consistent with the biblical testimony. But it is not an issue worth fighting over. Christians may disagree about the timing of end-time events, but nearly all agree on the big picture: There will be a rapture, and we will live forever with Jesus in heaven. In the long haul (after we've been with Christ for the equivalent of billions of years in heaven), the question of whether the rapture happened before or after the tribulation period will seem utterly ridiculous.

What is the support for the pretribulational view of the rapture?

Revelation 3:10 indicates that because the church in Philadelphia patiently endured trials, they would be kept from the actual hour of testing coming on the whole world. Christians will be kept from the future period of suffering.

Further, no Old Testament passage on the tribulation mentions the church (Deuteronomy 4:29-30; Jeremiah 30:4-11; Daniel 8:24-27; 12:1-2). Nor does any New Testament passage on the Tribulation mention the church (Matthew 13:30,39-42,48-50; 24:15-31; 1 Thessalonians 5:4-9; 2 Thessalonians 2:1-12; Revelation 4–18).

Scripture does affirm that some believers will live during the tribulation period. But pretribs believe these people *become* believers sometime after the rapture. Perhaps they become believers as a result of the ministry of the 144,000 Jewish believers introduced in Revelation 7 (who themselves apparently come to faith in Christ after the rapture).

The church is not appointed to wrath (Romans 5:9; 1 Thessalonians 1:9-10; 5:9). Therefore, the church cannot go through the "great day of their wrath" in the tribulation period (Revelation 6:17).

Finally, throughout Scripture, God always protects

His people before judgment falls (see 2 Peter 2:5-9). Enoch was translated before the judgment of the flood. Noah was in the ark before the judgment of the flood. The firstborn among the Hebrews in Egypt were sheltered by the blood of the Paschal Lamb before judgment fell. So too will the church be secured safely before judgment falls in the tribulation period.

What will the tribulation period be like?

The tribulation will be a definite period of time at the end of the age that will be characterized by great travail (Matthew 24:29-35). It will be of such severity that no period in history past or future will equal it (Matthew 24:21). It is called the time of Jacob's trouble, for it is a judgment on Messiah-rejecting Israel (Jeremiah 30:7; Daniel 12:1-4). The nations will also be judged for their sin and rejection of Christ (Isaiah 26:21; Revelation 6:15-17). The period will last seven years (Daniel 9:24,27).

Scripture indicates that this period will be characterized by wrath (Romans 1:18), judgment (Revelation 14:7), indignation (Isaiah 26:20-21 NASB), trial (Revelation 3:10), trouble (Jeremiah 30:7), destruction (Joel 1:15), darkness (Amos 5:18), desolation (Daniel 9:27), devastation (Isaiah 24:1-4), and punishment (Isaiah 24:20-21).

What is the timing of Daniel's 70 weeks (Daniel 9:25-27)?

In Daniel 9 God provided a prophetic timetable for

the nation of Israel. The prophetic clock began ticking with the command (by Persian king Cyrus) to restore and rebuild Jerusalem following its destruction by Babylon (Daniel 9:25). According to this verse, Israel's timetable was divided into 70 groups of 7 years, totaling 490 years.

The first 69 groups of seven years—or 483 years—counted the years "from the issuing of the decree to restore and rebuild Jerusalem until the Anointed One, the ruler, comes" (Daniel 9:25). The Anointed One, of course, is Jesus Christ. *Anointed One* means "Messiah." The day Jesus rode into Jerusalem to proclaim Himself Israel's Messiah was 483 years to the day after Cyrus' command to restore and rebuild Jerusalem.

At that point God's prophetic clock stopped. Daniel describes a gap between these 483 years and the final 7 years of Israel's prophetic timetable. Several events were to take place during this "gap," according to Daniel 9:26.

1. The Messiah would be killed.

2. The city of Jerusalem and its temple would be destroyed (this occurred in AD 70).

3. The Jews would encounter difficulty and hardship from that time on.

The final "week" of seven years will begin when the Antichrist confirms a covenant with Israel for seven years (Daniel 9:27). When this peace pact is signed, the seven-year tribulation period begins, followed by the second coming of Christ.

What is Christ's millennial kingdom?

There are three theological views regarding the millennial kingdom.

Premillennialism (the view I think is correct) says that following the second coming, Christ will institute a kingdom of perfect peace and righteousness on earth that will last for one thousand years. After this extended reign of true peace, the eternal state begins.

Amillennialism is the view that when Christ comes, the eternal state will begin with no prior thousand-year (millennial) reign on earth. Amillennialists generally interpret the thousand-year reign of Christ metaphorically and say it refers to Christ's present rule from heaven.

Postmillennialism says that through the church's influence, the world will be "Christianized" before Christ returns. Immediately following this return, the eternal state will begin.

I believe the premillennial view is most consistent with a literal interpretation of Scripture.

26

The Wonder of Heaven

What happens when we die?

The New Testament word for *death* carries the idea of separation. At the moment of physical death, man's spirit separates or departs from his body (Acts 7:59). "The spirit returns to God who gave it" (Ecclesiastes 12:7). Death for the believer involves his or her spirit departing from the physical body and immediately going into the presence of the Lord in heaven. That's why Paul could say, "For to me, to live is Christ and to die is gain" (Philippians 1:21).

For the unbeliever, however, death holds grim prospects. At death the unbeliever's spirit departs from the body and goes not to heaven but to a place of great suffering (Luke 16:19-31; 2 Peter 2:9).

Both believers and unbelievers remain as spirits (in a disembodied state) until the future day of resurrection. God will reunite believers' spirits with their resurrected and completely renewed physical bodies. These bodies will be specially suited to dwelling in heaven in the direct presence of God—the perishable will be made imperishable and the mortal will be made immortal (1 Corinthians 15:53). Unbelievers will also be resurrected, but they will spend eternity apart from God.

What are the three heavens?

The third heaven is the ineffable and glorious dwelling place of God in all His glory (2 Corinthians 12:2). It is also called the highest heaven (1 Kings 8:27; 2 Chronicles 2:6). The first heaven is the earth's atmosphere (Job 35:5). The second heaven is the stellar universe (Genesis 1:17 NASB; Deuteronomy 17:3 NASB).

What are the "old heaven and earth" and the "new heaven and earth"?

Adam and Eve's sin brought a curse on the earth (Genesis 3:17-18). So before God can manifest the eternal kingdom, He must renew this cursed earth along with the first and second heavens (the earth's atmosphere and the stellar universe).

The Scriptures often speak of the passing of the old heaven and earth. In the book of Revelation we read, "Then I saw a new heaven and a new earth, for the first heaven and the first earth had passed away, and there was no longer any sea...He who was seated on the throne said, 'I am making everything new!'" (Revelation 21:1,5).

The Greek word used to designate the newness of the cosmos is *kainos*. This word means "new in nature" or "new in quality." In other words, the phrase *a new heaven and a new earth* does not refer to a cosmos that is totally other than the present cosmos. Rather, the new cosmos will stand in continuity with the present cosmos, but it will be utterly renewed and renovated (see Matthew 19:28; Acts 3:21). The new heaven and the new earth will be brought into blessed conformity with all that God is in a state of fixed bliss and absolute perfection.

In the next life, heaven and earth will no longer be separate realms as they are now, but will be merged. Believers will thus continue to be in heaven even while they are on the new earth. The new earth will be utterly sinless and will be bathed and suffused in the light and splendor of

God, unobscured by evil of any kind or tarnished by evil-doers of any description (see Revelation 21).

If flesh and blood cannot enter God's kingdom, will our resurrection bodies not be physical (1 Corinthians 15:50)?

Our resurrection bodies will be physical. The term *flesh and blood* is simply an idiom used in Scripture to refer to mortal, perishable humanity. This verse is saying that mortal human beings in their present perishable bodies cannot inherit heaven. Mortal humanity must be made immortal humanity in order to survive in heaven. As 1 Corinthians 15:53 puts it, "The perishable must clothe itself with the imperishable, and the mortal with immortality."

What will Christians do for all eternity in heaven?

The book of Revelation portrays believers in the eternal state as offering worship and praise before the throne of God and Christ (Revelation 19:1-6). The worship that takes place in heaven will be ultimately fulfilling. We will virtually lose ourselves in the sheer joy of expressing the adoration and love we feel for God in our hearts.

We will also perpetually serve God and Christ (Revelation 1:5-6; 22:3). This will not be a tedious kind of service, but a joyous one—fully meeting our heart's every desire.

We will also reign with Christ. In Revelation 22:5 we are told that believers "will reign for ever and ever." We will be involved in some capacity in the heavenly government.

As well, our service will include judging the angels somehow (1 Corinthians 6:2-3). This is noteworthy because man at present is lower than the angels (see Psalm 8:5). The situation will be reversed in the eternal state. Angels will be lower than redeemed humanity in heaven.

We will also perpetually learn more about our glorious God. Throughout future ages believers will be shown "the incomparable riches of his grace" (Ephesians 2:7).

Do babies and little children go to heaven at the moment of death?

I believe the Scriptures teach that every infant who dies is immediately ushered into God's glorious presence in heaven. At the moment of death, Jesus applies the benefits of His death on the cross to that child, thereby saving him or her.

At the outset, we must recognize that the whole of Scripture points to the universal need of salvation—even among little children. All of us—including infants who cannot believe—are lost (Luke 19:10), perishing (John 3:16), condemned (John 3:18), and under God's wrath (John 3:36). In view of this, we cannot say that little children are in a sinless state. That is why it is necessary for Christ to apply the benefits of His death on the cross to each child who dies.

Scripture uniformly testifies that those who die without being capable of making a decision to receive Jesus Christ are now with Christ in heaven, resting in His tender arms, enjoying the sweetness of His love. Several factors support this viewpoint.

In all the biblical descriptions of hell, we never read of infants or little children there. Only adults capable of making decisions are seen there. Nor do we read of infants and little children standing before the great white throne, where the wicked dead are judged before being thrown into the lake of fire (Revelation 20:11-15).

Children seem to have a special place in Christ's kingdom. Jesus even said, "Unless you change and become like little children, you will never enter the kingdom of heaven" (Matthew 18:3). In the Old Testament, King David certainly believed he would again be with his young son who died (2 Samuel 12:22-23).

In John's vision of the great white throne, the lost were judged "according to what they had done." Infants cannot possibly be the objects of this judgment because they are not responsible for their deeds.

These and other Scriptural factors make it clear that babies and young children go straight to heaven at the moment of death.

Will we recognize our Christian loved ones in the afterlife?

Yes. The Thessalonian Christians were understandably concerned about their Christian loved ones who had died. They expressed their concern to the apostle Paul. So in 1 Thessalonians 4:13-17, Paul talks about those who have died in Christ and assures the Thessalonian Christians that a reunion awaits them. And yes, believers will recognize their loved ones in the eternal state.

We are told in 2 Samuel 12:23 that David knew he would be reunited with his deceased son in heaven. He had no doubt about recognizing him. As well, in Jesus' story of the rich man and Lazarus in Luke 16:19-31, all three characters—the rich man, Lazarus, and Abraham—recognized each other in the intermediate state.

How can we be happy in heaven knowing that people are suffering in hell?

This is a difficult question to answer. God may purge our memories. Isaiah 65:17 (NASB) tells us, "For behold, I create new heavens and a new earth, and the former things will not be remembered or come into mind."

Certainly God Himself has promised that He will take away all pain and remove all our tears (Revelation 21:4). The issue is in His hands. We can rest assured that God has the power and ability to do as He has promised. It is a fact that we will be happy in heaven. God has promised it.

27

The Judgment of Humankind

Will Christians stand before the judgment seat of Christ?

All believers will one day stand before the judgment seat of Christ (Romans 14:8-10; 2 Corinthians 5:10). At that time each believer's life will be examined in regard to the things done while in the body. Personal motives and intents of the heart will also be weighed.

The judgment seat refers to the athletic games of Paul's day. After the races and games concluded, the emperor himself often took his seat on an elevated throne, and each winning athlete approached the throne to receive his reward. This reward was usually a wreath of leaves, or a "victor's crown." When we Christians have finished our earthly race, each of us will stand before Christ the Judge and receive (or lose) rewards.

This judgment has nothing to do with going to heaven or hell. Those who have placed their faith in Christ are saved, and nothing threatens that. Believers are eternally secure in their salvation (Ephesians 4:30). Only believers will appear at this judgment, and they will simply receive or lose rewards (1 Corinthians 3:12-15).

What will Christians be judged on?

God will judge Christians' actions (Matthew 16:27). The psalmist said to the Lord, "Surely you will reward each person according to what he has done" (Psalm 62:12).

God will also scrutinize our thoughts. In Jeremiah 17:10 God said, "I the LORD search the heart and examine the mind, to reward a man according to his conduct, according to what his deeds deserve." The Lord "will bring to light what is hidden in darkness and will expose the motives of men's hearts" (1 Corinthians 4:5).

Finally, God will judge us for all the words we have spoken. Christ said that "men will have to give account on the day of judgment for every careless word they have spoken" (Matthew 12:36).

What kinds of rewards will believers receive at the judgment seat of Christ?

Scripture pictures our rewards as crowns.

The *crown of life* is given to those who persevere under trial, and especially to those who suffer to the point of death (James 1:12; Revelation 2:10).

The *crown of glory* is given to those who faithfully and sacrificially minister God's Word to the flock (1 Peter 5:4).

The *crown incorruptible* is given to those who win the race of temperance and self-control (1 Corinthians 9:25).

The *crown of righteousness* is given to those who long for the second coming of Christ (2 Timothy 4:8).

Revelation 4:10 shows believers casting their crowns before the throne of God in an act of worship and adoration. This teaches us something very important. Clearly we receive the crowns (our rewards) not for our own glory but ultimately for the glory of God. Believers are redeemed in order to bring glory to God (1 Corinthians

6:20). The act of placing our crowns before the throne of God seems to be an illustration of this.

What is the great white throne judgment?

The judgment at the great white throne is only for unbelievers (Revelation 20:11-15). Believers will not participate in this horrific judgment. Christ is the divine Judge, and He will judge the unsaved dead of all time. The judgment takes place at the end of the millennial kingdom, Christ's 1000-year reign on planet earth.

Those who face Christ at this judgment will be judged on the basis of their works (Revelation 20:12-13). It is critical to understand that they actually appear at this judgment because they are already unsaved. This judgment will not separate believers from unbelievers, for all who will experience it will have already made the choice during their lifetimes to reject God. Once they are before the divine Judge, they are judged according to their works not only to justify their condemnation but to determine the degree to which each person should be punished throughout eternity in hell.

Is hell real?

The Scriptures assure us that hell is a real place. But hell was not part of God's original creation, which He called good (Genesis 1). Hell was created later to accommodate the banishment of Satan and his fallen angels who rebelled against God (Matthew 25:41). Human beings who reject Christ will join Satan and his fallen angels in this infernal place of suffering.

One of the more important New Testament words for hell is *Gehenna* (for example, it is the Greek word used in Matthew 10:28.) This word has an interesting history. Near Jerusalem was a valley with a public rubbish dump, into which all the filth in Jerusalem was poured. Not only garbage but also the bodies of dead animals and the corpses of criminals were thrown on the heap where they—like everything else in the dump—would perpetually burn. The valley was a place where the fires never stopped burning. And there was always a good meal for a hungry worm. Idolatrous kings also used the valley for burning sacrifices to other gods (2 Kings 23:10).

This place was originally called (in the Hebrew) *Ge[gen]hinnom* (the valley of the sons of Hinnom). It was eventually shortened to the name *Ge-Hinnom*. The Greek translation of this Hebrew phrase is *Gehenna*. It became an appropriate and graphic term for the reality of hell. Jesus Himself used the word 11 times in the Gospels as a metaphorical way of describing the eternal place of suffering of unredeemed humanity.

Does God really send anyone to hell?

God does not want to send anyone to hell. That is why He sent Jesus—to pay the penalty for our sins by dying on the cross (John 3:16-17). Unfortunately, not all people are willing to admit that they sin and to place their faith in the Savior. They do not accept the payment of Jesus' death for them. So God lets them experience the results of their choice (see Luke 16:19-31).

C.S. Lewis once said that in the end there are two groups of people. One group of people says to God, "Thy will be done." These are those who have placed their faith in Jesus Christ and will live forever with God in heaven. The second group of people are those to whom God says, sadly, "Thy will be done!" These are those who have rejected Jesus Christ and will spend eternity apart from Him.

Is the fire of hell literal fire, or is this a metaphorical way of describing punishment?

Scholars are divided on this issue. Some believe the fire of hell is quite literal—and that may very well be the case. Others believe the fire is a metaphorical way of expressing the great wrath of God. Scripture tells us, "The LORD your God is a consuming fire, a jealous God" (Deuteronomy 4:24). "God is a consuming fire" (Hebrews 12:29). "His wrath is poured out like fire" (Nahum 1:6). "Who can stand when he appears? For he will be like a refiner's fire" (Malachi 3:2). God said, "My wrath will break out and burn like fire because of the evil you have done—burn with no one to quench it" (Jeremiah 4:4). Whether the fire of hell is literal or metaphorical, it will entail horrible suffering for those who are there.

Are there degrees of punishment in hell?

Yes. The degree of punishment will be commensurate with people's sin against the light they have received. Consider Luke 12:47-48:

That servant who knows his master's will and does not get ready or does not do what his master wants will be beaten with many blows. But the one who does not know and does things deserving punishment will be beaten with few blows. From everyone who has been given much, much will be demanded; and from the one who has been entrusted with much, much more will be asked.

Other verses on this issue include Matthew 10:15; 16:27; Revelation 20:12-13; 22:12.

Will the punishment of the wicked in hell be an eternal punishment, or is it temporary?

Jesus affirmed that the wicked "will go away to eternal punishment, but the righteous to eternal life" (Matthew 25:46). Notice that the eternality of the punishment of the wicked equals the eternality of the eternal life of the righteous. One is just as long as the other. The punishment of the wicked never ceases.

The eternal nature of this punishment is emphasized all throughout Scripture. The fire of hell, for example, "never goes out" (Mark 9:43); the "smoke of [sinners'] torment rises for ever and ever" (Revelation 14:11).

Let Us Not Forget...

- The Word of God is living (Hebrews 4:12-13).
- The Word of God is absolutely true (John 17:17).
- The Word of God is utterly trustworthy (Psalm 111:7).
- The Word of God gives us light (Psalm 19:8; 119:105,130; Proverbs 6:23; 2 Peter 1:19).
- The Word of God perpetually teaches us what we need to know (Deuteronomy 4:10; 2 Chronicles 17:9).
- The Word of God feeds our souls (Deuteronomy 8:3; Job 23:12; Psalm 119:103; Jeremiah 15:16).
- The Word of God gives us perpetual hope (Romans 15:4).
- The Word of God keeps us from sinning (Psalm 119:9-16).
- The Word of God purifies us (Psalm 119:9; John 17:17; Ephesians 5:25-26; 1 Peter 1:22).
- The Word of God never passes away (Matthew 24:35).

Bibliography

Ankerberg, John, and John Weldon. *The Facts on False Teaching in the Church*. Eugene, OR: Harvest House, 1988.

———. *The Facts on Life After Death*. Eugene, OR: Harvest House, 1992.

Arndt, William. *Bible Difficulties and Seeming Contradictions*. St. Louis, MO: Concordia, 1987.

Basinger, David, and Randall Basinger, eds. *Predestination and Free Will: Four Views of Divine Sovereignty and Human Freedom*. Downers Grove, IL: InterVarsity Press, 1986.

Barker, Kenneth, ed. *The NIV Study Bible*. Grand Rapids, MI: Zondervan, 1985.

Barker, Kenneth L., and John Kohlenberger, eds. *Zondervan NIV Bible Commentary*. Grand Rapids, MI: Zondervan, 1994.

Bruce, F.F. *The Hard Sayings of Jesus*. Downers Grove, IL: InterVarsity Press, 1983.

Campbell, Donald K., ed. *Walvoord: A Tribute*. Chicago, IL: Moody Press, 1982.

Davids, Peter. *More Hard Sayings of the New Testament*. Downers Grove, IL: InterVarsity Press, 1991.

Elwell, Walter A., ed. *The Concise Evangelical Dictionary of Theology*. Grand Rapids, MI: Baker, 1991.

Geisler, Norman. *Ethics: Alternatives and Issues*. Grand Rapids, MI: Zondervan, 1979.

———, ed. *Inerrancy*. Grand Rapids, MI: Zondervan, 1980.

Geisler, Norman, and Ron Rhodes. *Correcting the Cults*. Grand Rapids, MI: Baker, 2004.

Geisler, Norman, and Ronald Brooks. *When Skeptics Ask*. Wheaton, IL: Victor Books, 1990.

Geisler, Norman, and Thomas Howe. *When Critics Ask: A Popular Handbook on Bible Difficulties*. Wheaton, IL: Victor Books, 1992.

Geisler, Norman, and William Nix. *A General Introduction to the Bible*. Chicago, IL: Moody Press, 1978.

Gomes, Alan W. *Unmasking the Cults*. Grand Rapids, MI: Zondervan, 1995.

Ham, Ken. *The Lie*. El Cajon, CA: Creation-Life, 1987.

Henry, Carl F.H., ed. *Baker's Dictionary of Christian Ethics*. Grand Rapids, MI: Baker, 1978.

Hoyt, Herman A. *The End Times*. Chicago, IL: Moody Press, 1969.

Kaiser, Walter. *Hard Sayings of the Old Testament*. Downers Grove, IL: InterVarsity Press, 1988.

———. *More Hard Sayings of the Old Testament*. Downers Grove, IL: InterVarsity Press, 1992.

Kreeft, Peter, and Ronald Tacelli. *Handbook of Christian Apologetics*. Downers Grove, IL: InterVarsity Press, 1994.

Lightner, Robert. *Evangelical Theology. A Survey and Review*. Grand Rapids, MI: Baker, 1986.

———. *The God of the Bible*. Grand Rapids, MI: Baker, 1978.

———. *The Last Days Handbook*. Nashville, TN: Thomas Nelson, 1990.

Mather, George, and Larry A. Nichols. *Dictionary of Cults, Sects, Religions and the Occult*. Grand Rapids, MI: Zondervan, 1993.

McDowell, Josh. *The Resurrection Factor*. San Bernardino, CA: Here's Life, 1981.

McDowell, Josh, and Don Stewart. *Answers to Tough Questions Skeptics Ask About the Christian Faith*. Wheaton, IL: Tyndale House, 1988.

———. *Handbook of Today's Religions*. San Bernardino, CA: Here's Life, 1989.

———. *Reasons Skeptics Should Consider Christianity*. Wheaton, IL: Tyndale House, 1988.

O'Brien, David. *Today's Handbook for Solving Bible Difficulties*. Minneapolis, MN: Bethany House, 1990.

Rhodes, Ron. *Angels Among Us: Separating Truth from Fiction*. Eugene, OR: Harvest House, 2007.

————. *Christ Before the Manger: The Life and Times of the Preincarnate Christ*. Grand Rapids, MI: Baker, 1992.

————. *The Wonder of Heaven*. Eugene, OR: Harvest House, 2009.

Ryrie, Charles C. *Balancing the Christian Life*. Chicago, IL: Moody Press, 1969.

————. *Basic Theology*. Wheaton, IL: Victor Books, 1986.

————. *Dispensationalism Today*. Chicago, IL: Moody Press, 1977.

————. *The Holy Spirit*. Chicago, IL: Moody Press, 1988.

————. *You Mean the Bible Teaches That…* Chicago, IL: Moody Press, 1974.

————, ed. *Ryrie Study Bible*. Chicago, IL: Moody Press, 1994.

Saucy, Robert. *The Church in God's Program*. Chicago, IL: Moody Press, 1972.

Sire, James. *Scripture Twisting: 20 Ways the Cults Misread the Bible*. Downers Grove, IL: InterVarsity Press, 1980.

Stein, Robert. *Difficult Passages in the New Testament*. Grand Rapids, MI: Baker, 1990.

Story, Dan. *Defending Your Faith: How to Answer the Tough Questions*. Nashville, TN: Thomas Nelson, 1992.

Walvoord, John F. *Jesus Christ Our Lord*. Chicago, IL: Moody Press, 1969.

————. *The Prophecy Knowledge Handbook*. Wheaton, IL: Victor Books, 1990.

————. *The Rapture Question*. Grand Rapids, MI: Zondervan, 1979.

Walvoord, John F., and Roy B. Zuck, eds. *The Bible Knowledge Commentary: New Testament*. Wheaton, IL: Victor Books, 1983.

————, eds. *The Bible Knowledge Commentary: Old Testament*. Wheaton, IL: Victor Books, 1985.

Youngblood, Ronald, ed. *Nelson's New Illustrated Bible Dictionary*. Nashville, TN: Thomas Nelson, 1995.

Subject Index

Scripture Index

The 10 Most Important Things Series

The 10 Most Important Things
You Can Say to a Catholic

The 10 Most Important
Things You Can Say to
a Jehovah's Witness

The 10 Most Important Things
You Can Say to a Mason

The 10 Most Important Things
You Can Say to a Mormon

The Reasoning from the Scriptures Series

Reasoning from the
Scriptures with Catholics

Reasoning from the Scriptures
with the Jehovah's Witnesses

Reasoning from the
Scriptures with Masons

Reasoning from the
Scriptures with the Mormons

Reasoning from the
Scriptures with Muslims

Quick Reference Guides

Archaeology and the Bible:
What You Need to Know

Christian Views of War:
What You Need to Know

Five Views on the Rapture:
What You Need to Know

Halloween: What You
Need to Know

Homosexuality: What
You Need to Know

Is America in Bible Prophecy?:
What You Need to Know

Islam: What You Need to Know

Jehovah's Witnesses: What
You Need to Know

The Middle East Conflict: What
You Need to Know